ROAR!

How to Tame the Bully Inside and Out

Marilise de Villiers Basson

RETHINK PRESS

First published in Great Britain in 2019 by
Rethink Press (www.rethinkpress.com)

© Copyright Marilise de Villiers Basson

Cover and illustrations by Christi du Toit: www.christidutoit.co.za

PRAISE

'This is a bold, positive and impactful book that pulls no punches. It shines a light on an issue many suffer with in silence: workplace bullying. It is an issue almost all of us have witnessed, if not been affected by in some way, shape or form. *ROAR!* doesn't just deal with the external challenges people face but addresses the all-important internal challenges too. In doing so, it champions kindness, consideration for others, high performance and positive drive. These are all traits we need in greater measure across society. This book can help us all.'

— **Lt Col (Retd) Oz Alashe MBE**, CEO and founder of CybSafe and former UK Special Forces officer

'Full to bursting with compelling stories, practical tips and constructive nudges, *ROAR!* creates a world where you can flourish and be whomever you want to be – led by the ultimate role model in inspiration and creativity herself, Marilise de Villiers. Be kind and give yourself permission to be the best version of you. Embrace the energy, experience and warmth offered in this book. We all need to hear our ROAR.'

— **Tracey Groves**, CEO, Intelligent Ethics

'Reading *ROAR!* was like inhaling oxygen – stimulating my mind and raising my emotions. The book inspires the understanding that it is not about the bully that attacks us, or being the victim enabled by our self-criticism, or the culture that causes it to flourish. It is about overcoming adversity. It is about accepting ourselves, choosing to be the best self we can be and loving the one we are.'

— **Audra Simons**, Director, Forcepoint Innovation Labs

'A business book that captivates you like the best novel. This is a must read for any business person struggling because they are being bullied, or to ensure they do not unintentionally become the bully. I enjoyed the sound and practical advice and understanding of what makes a bully a bully!'

— **Sarah Janes**, CEO, Layer 8

'Choosing to follow the path of our best life is what Marilise encourages us to do. In ROAR! she gives us an honest account of overcoming a very difficult situation. We all have a starting point, a pivotal moment in our lives where we choose to step up, play a bigger game, be brave and follow our heart. ROAR! is a story of how to do this with passion, purpose and commitment.

Marilise shines a light on this emotive topic brilliantly, sharing her experiences and life lessons to help us tame the bully. Don't try to 'eat the elephant' in one go; follow her step-by-step model and let her show you how to trust in your ability to figure things out, and how to commit to living your best life. I hope you find this book as inspirational as I have.'

— **Colette Pienaar**, transformation coach and founder of The Goddess Academy

'If you hold an aspiration to live your best life then Marilise is the perfect guide to help you on your way. This wonderfully digestible book will help you see yourself and those around you. It will give you the power to evolve towards a kinder, stronger, more compassionate self, not just for you but for everyone.

— **Andy Woodfield**, partner, PwC

'If you are being bullied, simply buy *ROAR!* – right now! It's going to hand you the fast-track secrets you need to move forward to a place of confident empowerment. Marilise has elegantly woven in her raw stories of adversity and shared the tools – scientifically proven and research-backed – that, through her journey and those of others, are proven to work – when you put in the work. This book uncovers the incredible journey you can make to higher levels of personal success through your kind interaction with yourself and others.'

— **Natasha Mogg-Addis**, CHPC, international leadership coach and founder of NM Consulting

'Having had to create my own strategies to deal with my scars from childhood, corporate and social bullying, it was a delight to read *ROAR!* You are provided with a down-to-earth look at bullying, full of tips and strategies to help you protect yourself and go beyond the bullying. Special insights include sections on the bullying from within oneself, and how to develop a mindset and lifestyle that will help you move from being bullied to living an abundant life.

I thoroughly loved reading *ROAR!* and would recommend it to everyone working within the corporate and entrepreneurial world.'

— **Ben Chai**, author, entrepreneur and TEDx speaker

'Although we may not like to admit it, bullying doesn't stop when you leave school. Workplace bullying is rife and even if you haven't been at the sharp end of it, you've witnessed it at some point. But what can you do? Full of practical advice and guidance, this book will help you understand your options and plan a way forward – whether you're a victim, an observer or an HR manager. I just wish I'd had access to this book throughout my professional career.'

— **Steve Thorne**, retired cyber security executive

'*ROAR!* comes from the heart, is grounded in evidence and full of practical advice on what to do about this corrosive force in the workplace. It has great advice for anyone dealing with a bully alone, and I hope HR leaders read it closely to understand the impact that tolerating bullying behaviours has on their staff. Marilise offers great support for victims but places the responsibility for solving the problem where it needs to be – with perpetrators, and the organisations that protect them.'

— **Melissa Sabella**, founder and CEO, The Honeycomb Works

'*ROAR!* is a work of inspiration about overcoming fear and challenges, not only at work, but also in our personal lives – challenges that most of us have experienced at some point but didn't quite know how to deal with. I identified with many of the situations and self-limiting beliefs written about in the book. Fortunately, *ROAR!* has provided me with clear, concise and, importantly, practical advice and methods to help shift my mindset so I can approach difficult situations with a positive and healthy attitude.'

— **Zsuzsanna Berenyi**, cyber security awareness specialist

'Marilise has written her book from the heart with a real desire to help others find their path through difficult times at work and at home. She writes with authenticity, based on principles founded in solid research, about issues we can all recognise. We have all been there and experienced the bully. If you are in a position to want to read this you will need tissues, but you will emerge a stronger person.

— **Carolyn Clarke**, finance executive and Chair of Care International UK

'*ROAR!* takes you on a moving, brave and personal journey where achieving a fulfilled life is the ultimate goal. It encourages you to be true to yourself, to identify pain points, and gives you tools to see and embrace change. *ROAR!* battles conformism. It empowers you to be your best self and provides brilliant tips to create inner and outer "bully alerts" along the way. A must read, through which the author will take you on an exciting and inspiring tour to define your purpose and pursue your best life.'

— **Maria Isidro**, tech content and community engagement specialist

'ROAR! is one of the most authentic and genuine books I've ever read. It's applicable to so many aspects of life, making it very relatable. Marilise writes with pure determination and passion. As a twenty-one-year-old student pursuing a corporate career, I now have my own "warrior girl" guide to weather the inevitable storms coming my way. A must read for everyone – young and old.'

— **Mia du Toit**, student, blogger and fashionista

To Heinie, for the gift of unconditional love and kindness.
Without you none of this would be possible.
I love you and I appreciate you.

CONTENTS

FOREWORD

I am staggered by the amount of workplace bullying I hear about. You know the thing, where you hear about something once, then two, then three times, and you start to take notice. This is such an important topic, which Marilise meets head-on, drawing on painfully personal experience.

She calls it the 'silent epidemic' because people usually find it incredibly difficult to know how to deal with bullies in their organisations. They often leave without being honest about what was really happening, feeling grateful just to move as far away from the bully as possible. Or they stick it out because they need the job. Or they try and have the conversations internally and are met with disbelief or further bullying.

ROAR! is a brilliant acronym to help you deal with difficult situations when they arise. Marilise's disarmingly personal account of abuse in her lifetime, and her former belief that she was a 'bully magnet', will help you to speak out if you are suffering any form of bullying... whether you are doing this bullying to yourself, or others are doing it to you. If you follow the clear guidelines in the book, it will help you take ownership of your destiny and set you free.

Filled with practical tools and advice on how to recognise a bully and have those difficult conversations, *ROAR!* will help you understand the bullying mindset far better than ever before. Grounded in powerful research, this book is helpful for employees, employers, indeed, for anyone being held back from being the best version of themselves.

It is inspiring, thought-provoking and tender. It will help you to win the inner and outer game and inspire you to be your authentic self. Bringing more kindness to our world is the beautiful, central theme. Interestingly, the great Roald Dahl, when asked what the greatest human value was, said 'kindness'.

Now here is Marilise, the epitome of kindness, sharing with you her experience and wisdom, to help you tame the bully inside and out.

Be brave, and good luck. You now have the best guide and resources.

Ali Stewart, Ali Stewart & Co Ltd
Author, leadership coach and mentor
Founder of the accrediting body for Liberating Leadership® and
Pioneering Professional®

INTRODUCTION

'If you have the choice between being right and being kind, choose being kind.'

WAYNE DYER

During my forty-two years on this planet, I've never felt so strongly about the need for more kindness in our world; kindness to others and kindness to ourselves. We live in a picture-perfect, selfie-obsessed world where our every move is instantly scrutinised. Cyberbullying is on the rise – and the one thing that keeps me (as a parent) awake at night.

At work, I see too many people 'going through the motions' every day and I am not surprised that only 15% of workers, are highly engaged, according to global analytics firm Gallup.[1] This is a massive barrier to creating high-performing cultures and concerns me a lot. Unfortunately, all it often takes is a bad boss or an obnoxious co-worker to turn a job you love into a nightmare.

---

1   Gallup (2017) *State of the Global Workplace*, www.gallup.com/workplace/238079/state-global-workplace-2017.aspx#formheader

Just when I thought I had it all figured out, with things finally falling into place – family, work and relationships – I crossed paths with a workplace bully who brought me to my knees. My nightmare went on for almost four years as I dealt with a boss who bullied me and everyone else. At his mercy and fearing for our jobs, day in and day out we desperately tried to justify his mood swings, his rage, his 'my way or the highway' dictatorship. Those who left did so in silence, too scared to risk ruining their reputations by speaking up and too exhausted to fight any more.

It was this experience that inspired my book; in many ways it was the worst and best thing that could have happened to me. The biggest truth I had to face was my own role in all of this; the knowledge that I was partly to blame. I allowed my bully to become an energy vampire, sucking the lifeblood out of me, and in my attempt to please him and prove my worth – trying to fix problems that weren't fixable – I started bullying myself. That's why this book is about taming the bully inside and out. My inner bully is the 'all or nothing, people-pleasing' kind and although it mostly serves me with determination and grit, some days it also cripples me with fear, self-limiting beliefs and self-doubt. These are the days when I have to dig deep and remember to go easy on myself. If I don't, everyone else suffers too.

Only a small group of my family and friends have walked this path with me. It has been painful and self-destructive at times, but now I owe it to the world to share my story.

WHY I WROTE THIS BOOK

My aim is to shine a light on workplace bullying, which is still largely a silent epidemic – dare I say a silent killer – in the workplace today. I want people to understand the dynamics that play out when people demean, derail and destruct.

There is always a toxic trio: a bully, a victim, and a workplace culture that is a breeding ground for bullying behaviour.

Each member of the toxic trio needs to take responsibility for their actions (or inaction). This is why I focus on what all three have in common, instead of our differences. I position narcissism – the desire to feel special – as something we all need a healthy dose of, in order to turn our dreams into reality. However, when the behaviour becomes toxic – when there is a strong sense of entitlement present, or worse, a willingness to exploit others to win at all costs – it creates all sorts of problems, and this is where the victim almost always draws the short straw.

I want victims and bystanders to be able to recognise bullying behaviour when it occurs, and to be able to distinguish between someone being demanding versus being demeaning. Most importantly, I want people to find the inner strength and courage to call the behaviour out – either in the moment or soon afterwards – and do it in a way that will not get the bully's back up or throw fuel on the fire. It's much easier said than done, I know, but without it the bully will get away with demeaning others and will do it again and again until it becomes the norm, simply 'the way we do things around here', and destroying lives in the process.

It took me years to be able to spot workplace bullies. When you enter the corporate world straight out of university, you do whatever it takes to get the job done, to impress and progress, even if it means that you have to throw people under the bus in the process. When this clashes with your own beliefs and values, the inner turmoil and conflict can become soul destroying. I've worked with many 'accidental bullies' over the years – sometimes it's even been me – but it was only when I crossed paths with an extreme bully that I realised how toxic and destructive they are, and how universally bad they are for business. That is why I am on a mission to bring more kindness into the workplace. It is my dream that workplace bullying becomes socially unacceptable and frowned upon like all other forms of abuse.

Join me on my mission to tame the bully inside and out.

MY WORKPLACE CULTURE SURVEY

I ran a global survey comprising thirty-two questions (see My Workplace Culture Survey Questions at the end of the book) to support my research. As you will see, the results back up my conclusions. The survey results are based on 292 respondents across twenty-three countries (mainly Europe, South Africa, Australia and America).

CAVEAT

I am not a psychologist or a psychiatrist. Everything in this book is based on my own experience and the experiences of others. Nothing in this book constitutes professional or medical advice and should not be treated as such, but I can say that I've 'been there, done that'; I have become an expert through experience.

WHO IS THIS BOOK FOR?

Your best life is on the other side of your biggest obstacle. If you are ready to face it – no matter what – then this book is right for you. It aims to inspire, and by telling you my very personal story I hope that you'll see that if I can do it, so can you.

Although the focus of this book is on workplace bullying, at heart it is about overcoming adversity in general – those inevitable curveballs that life throws at you. In my case, it was the sexual abuse I suffered as an eight-year-old and the eating disorder that landed me in rehab. This was followed, many years later, by encountering a workplace bully whose mental and emotional abuse nearly destroyed me.

Just as I decided to go to rehab all those years ago, I decided to leave a toxic work relationship. I was at rock bottom but I saw a flickering of hope. Somehow, I took control and started my new journey. I was stunned to realise just how widespread and rife workplace bullying is, and so I decided to write this book.

When I started writing it was all about my boss – my personal bully – but it has become so much more. It is also about me and my inner bully. I realised just how much a lifetime of fear, self-limiting beliefs and low self-esteem had contributed to the toxic situation I found myself in. I was not letting my bully off the hook but I had to take responsibility for my part in the experience. Initially this was a bitter pill to swallow, but the realisation also set me free. I was able to let the bully go almost instantly.

It is my hope that you will be inspired to take action. Read this book once, then read it again. Use it as a practical guide to which you can refer. Even if you take the smallest action, it will be worth it, I promise. Most importantly, I want you to give yourself permission to pursue your best life. You will need to be realistic; Rome wasn't built in a day. It takes time to create great things. Take it one day at a time and stay focused no matter what – it's all about consistency and relentless pursuit. It's OK (inevitable, even) to relapse and fall back into old habits; just try to get yourself back on the right track as quickly as possible. Catch yourself early and try not to negotiate with yourself.

HOW TO USE THIS BOOK

As a visual learner, I need to be given pictures or to create my own. That is why this book is supported by images to capture the imagination of my readers. In the same way that my great-grandmother Susara du Toit de la Guerre[2] used to dream her paintings before painting them, I imagine and visualise what I want to write or say before I put pen to paper or create presentation aids.

For me, creativity and effective communication is everything – the ability to think outside the box and connect dots. I am passionate about turning words and complex concepts into meaningful and simple pictorial summaries, and even works of art. It is hard to describe in words how much this excites me. The day I created my 'Your best life' model (introduced in Chapter Four) was a turning point for me. The moment I designed the model, which is a 'signature diagram' and essentially a summary of the book, I knew exactly how this book would unfold. Even if you do nothing else, familiarise yourself with my 'Your best life' model.

Effective communication forms an integral part of my model and that's why I've also created a four-step process called ROAR (Recognise, Observe, Assert, Redirect) to help you approach difficult conversations with clarity and confidence. Imagine yourself as a lion (or lioness) asserting your position and making it known to others around you. When I encourage you to ROAR, I don't necessarily mean a loud, thundering sound, like Mufasa in *The Lion King* arriving to fight off a pack of hyenas; it could be something more subtle.

---

2   www.facebook.com/The-life-and-art-of-Susara-du-Toit-de-la-Guerre-174451392590321

It doesn't matter how you decide to ROAR, as long as it's authentic and you manage to defuse the situation. Ideally you should move the conversation towards mutual benefit and 'win-win' outcomes. What does matter is that you try it next time someone is rude to you. Then keep trying, and if you've tried a few times without any success, be honest with yourself and ask for help.

ONE

WORKPLACE BULLYING: A SILENT EPIDEMIC

'I've learned that people will forget what you said, people will forget what you did, but people will never forget how you made them feel.'

MAYA ANGELOU

The day I left my job – because of a bully – I was broken. I felt like a failure and the only person this had ever happened to. Ashamed and in denial, I was unable to say the words 'I was bullied' out loud. Much like twenty years ago when I was unable to utter the words 'I have an eating disorder'.

How on earth did I get myself back to this very dark place?

Fortunately, I got out before it killed me. For the second time, I started the long, painful journey of recovery. In the weeks that followed, the biggest eye opener was realising that I was not alone. Almost every person I spoke to – men and women I admire and respect – had their own story of experiencing workplace bullying at some point in their career, whether by a toxic boss, a co-worker or a subordinate. These conversations highlighted just how frighteningly common and costly workplace bullying is.

This was further evidenced in my global research study on workplace culture, where 77% of people said they had either been a target, witnessed bullying, or both. Roughly 40% of the targets were men.

You may not be ready to accept that you are being bullied, but for me, in order to get to the point where I could actually say it, I had to be honest with myself. Not only had I been bullied by someone else, I had also bullied myself – hence the subtitle of this book. This sentiment will make more sense as my story unfolds.

WHAT IS WORKPLACE BULLYING?

According to the Workplace Bullying Institute it is the 'repeated, health-harming mistreatment of one or more persons (the targets) by one or more perpetrators. It is abusive conduct that is:

- Threatening, humiliating, or intimidating, or

- Work interference – sabotage – which prevents work from getting done, or

- Verbal abuse'[3]

What's more, the abuse does seem to roll downhill. Workplace bullies are often in positions of power and abuse that power, 'kissing up and kicking down'. Respondents to my survey indicated that in 97% of cases, the bully was more senior or a peer with the same rank as the target. Roughly 32% of the bullies were women.

---

3   Workplace Bullying Institute (2014) 'The WBI Definition of Workplace Bullying', www.workplacebullying.org/individuals/problem/definition

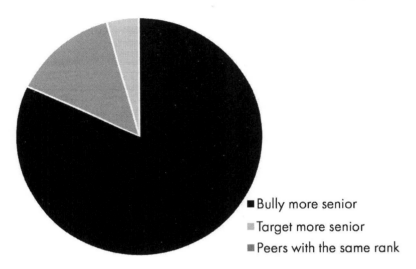

- ■ Bully more senior
- ▨ Target more senior
- ■ Peers with the same rank

MY STORY

I walked an almost four-year journey with my bully. At the time there were months in which every day was filled with anxiety. I struggled to sleep because I couldn't see a way out. I loved my team and didn't want to leave them, I needed the money, and it is not in my nature to quit. The thought of leaving without achieving my goals ripped my soul apart. I felt like a complete and utter failure. All I wanted to do was run and hide.

Shortly after I left, a friend asked me, 'Why on earth didn't you leave sooner?' Her question caught me completely off guard. Red-faced and irritated (I mean, how dare she? Did she have no idea what I'd been going through?), I replied defensively, 'It's complex,' then continued with some lengthy rationale of why I did what I did or, in fact, didn't do. It felt like the toughest question to answer at the time, and I wasn't ready to answer it honestly.

Fast forward a few years, and I am now ready to answer this question. At least I was right about one thing: it is complex. At the time, I just didn't realise quite *how* complex.

MY FIVE REASONS FOR STAYING PUT

1. I didn't realise I was being bullied
2. I thought I was the problem
3. I enjoyed the job status and needed the money
4. I was loyal and my team needed me
5. I had no one to voice my concerns to

Let's delve into each a bit more.

Please note: I go much deeper into my personal story in each chapter; this is just to set the scene and give you a flavour of the experience I had with my bully, which was also the inspiration behind this book.

1. I didn't realise I was being bullied

For almost two years, I honestly didn't realise I was being bullied. When we first started working together, the bully – my boss – was charismatic and inspired confidence in me. He boosted my self-esteem and made me feel like I was a key individual in his winning team. This stroked my ambitious (and somewhat narcissistic) ego. On reflection, I think it is safe to say that I was being 'played'. While my admiration and interest in him was quite genuine, I only realised (too late) that his was fake. I was merely a stepping stone for him to advance his career.

It became a rollercoaster ride: one day he would be a great boss to work for, only to turn into Mr Hyde the next. The highs compensated for the lows. But the most stressful thing, and probably my biggest 'energy suck', was the constant guessing game of 'will he be in a good or bad mood today?' Just the thought of walking past his office triggered my anxiety attacks and nearly destroyed me towards the end.

2. I thought I was the problem

For a very long time, I genuinely thought that I was the problem. I was still finding my feet in cybersecurity, and one day one of the experts in my team told me, 'Marilise, you are not technical and therefore will never be taken seriously.' I went on a mission to prove him wrong, but deep down I believed him. He was right: I didn't feel good enough.

Perhaps the most obvious sign was that I started my conversations with 'I am not technical, but...' Eventually I realised that I didn't need to prove my colleague wrong; I had to convince *myself* that I was good enough.

With the benefit of hindsight, I can now see how the bullying reignited my own destructive patterns of past behaviour: anxiety, low self-esteem, a constant need for external validation, a lack of boundaries and self-sabotage. My past influenced the present.

At the age of twelve, after exposing the man who sexually abused me (and a bunch of other kids in the neighbourhood), I obsessively threw myself into exercise. It didn't take me long to develop an unhealthy relationship with food too. I became addicted to the control I had over both. By over-exercising and starving myself I blocked off my feelings of shame. We lived in a very small town in the countryside called Bredasdorp; everybody knew what had happened, and I felt like damaged goods. I eventually became bulimic and very manipulative, doing whatever it took to protect my eating disorder. It took me another fifteen years and a stint in rehab to recover fully.

I will come back to this experience later in the book when I talk about the importance of winning the inner game (your thoughts and feelings) and the outer game (your words and actions), but I mention it now because my experience with a bully at work felt like a repeat of the abuse I suffered as a child. Although the bullying wasn't physical, it had the same emotional impact on me. The destructive characteristics – the anxiety, low self-esteem, a constant need for external validation, a lack of boundaries and negative self-talk – re-emerged. I instinctively knew that I had to find a healthy way of dealing with my feelings of shame – mainly about tolerating and normalising the bully's behaviour. Just the thought of my eating disorder resurfacing was petrifying.

This was my second chance, and this time around I owed it to my husband, my sons and, above all, to myself to be healthy. I decided to get into the best shape of my life, mentally and physically. For the first time in my life I hired a coach to help me with my nutrition, exercise and mindset.

You'll read more about my mindset and body transformation in Chapters Six and Seven.

3. I enjoyed the job status and needed the money

As a self-confessed career woman, I've worked relentlessly to climb the 'corporate ladder'. For a long time, I defined success as becoming a partner in a Big Four accounting firm; until circumstances changed, and I was gently 'kicked out of the nest'. The new job was a fantastic opportunity; I was told that I was key to the future success of my new organisation. This was all very flattering, and I enjoyed the job status. Also, with a young family to provide for, I needed the money, which was decent.

4. I was loyal and my team needed me

I also felt that I had to protect my team and act as a sort of buffer between them and the bully. One day, out of the blue, he told me, 'Marilise, you need to decide where your loyalty lies, whether it is with the team or with me, because you know,' he said, pointing towards himself, 'where the decisions are made.'

5. I had no one to voice my concerns to

For a very long time I suffered in silence, and this was largely down to my self-sabotage. As discussed earlier, I thought that I was the problem. My organisation's HR policies and procedures – or rather lack thereof – allowed my bully to get away with murder (well, almost).

I'll talk more about organisational cultures and the role of HR in the next chapter.

THE DAY I SAW THE WRITING ON THE WALL

After months of feeling like I was fighting battle after battle, it became clear that I was not going to be allowed to lead and develop my team towards high performance. When I saw the writing on the wall, I knew a 'divorce' was inevitable. I had to leave my job. I wanted to run, and at the same time, to leave things as they were. I even thought that I'd stay as I couldn't see a way out. That would have been the biggest mistake of my life.

I remember to this day that sinking feeling when I realised that there was nothing I could do any more to 'fix' the situation. I felt physically ill. By then I was suffering anxiety attacks daily, I was struggling to sleep, and my body was piling on weight, which was largely down to exhaustion, stress and drinking too much. I realised that the price I was paying was too high. I was at rock bottom, mentally and physically exhausted, and my relationships with the most important people in my life were suffering a great deal as a result.

That day, when he demoted me in front of my entire team, it felt like being punched in the stomach. I barely made it to the bathroom where I cried my eyes out. Deep down a little voice inside me said, 'That's it. You're done.' I finally listened. I quit the next day and started a slow, painful process of recovery. It all started when I took back my power, when I decided that enough was enough.

I want the same for you. I sincerely hope that my story and the guidance in this book empower and compel you to take action. I want you to take back your power and say: 'Enough is enough. I deserve better.'

INTRODUCING NARCISSISM

In my attempt to understand my bully's destructive behaviour, and my own, I started doing research on personality disorders, which quickly led me to narcissism. These days, we're so quick to label someone a 'narcissist' – it's become a bit of a buzzword. What does it really mean?

TYPES OF NARCISSIST

Perhaps unsurprisingly, it turns out that my initial view of a narcissist largely describes a bullying narcissist, so someone who:

- Builds themselves up by humiliating other people
- Relies on contempt to make others feel inferior
- Belittles and mocks you
- Becomes threatening when they need something from you

At their most toxic, bullying narcissists make you doubt yourself and your value as a human being.

I discovered the work of Dr Joseph Burgo online and asked him about the difference between a bully and a narcissist. He replied: 'All bullies are narcissists. Not all narcissists are bullies, but many are.'[4] I started delving deeper to improve my understanding of narcissism.

Its definition is alarmingly vague for a word that is used an awful lot to hurl insults at people who appear to have an excessive sense of self: self-admiration, self-centredness, self-importance, vanity and a need for attention. In its most extreme form, narcissism is a mental illness called narcissistic personality disorder (NPD). This is a clinical diagnosis as defined by the American Psychiatric Association. The *Diagnostic and Statistical Manual of Mental Disorders* (DSM-5)[5] describes nine

---

4   Burgo, J (2013) 'All Bullies Are Narcissists', *The Atlantic*, 14 November, www.theatlantic.com/health/archive/2013/11/all-bullies-are-narcissists/281407
5   www.psychiatry.org/psychiatrists/practice/dsm

criteria and if a person is diagnosed (after extensive therapy and observation by a qualified psychiatrist) with five or more of the nine, they have NPD.

The narcissists we encounter may or may not have NPD, but it is not our job to diagnose them. Very few ever seek help – they deny they have a problem – which means many are never diagnosed.

It is estimated that extreme narcissists (those who meet four of the nine DSM-5 criteria), make up an astonishing 5–10% of the world's population.[6] They are not just vain, irritating individuals who think a little too highly of themselves; they are outright dangerous.

In addition to the bullying narcissist (described above), there are many different types of extreme narcissists,[7] including:

- **Know-it-all narcissists** believe their opinion – on any topic – matters more than anyone else's, even if unsolicited. Know-it-all narcissists like to talk at people and are terrible listeners because they're thinking about what they want to say next.

- **Grandiose narcissists** believe they're more important and influential than everyone else – that they are destined for great things – and are obsessed with eliciting envy or admiration. They flaunt their own accomplishments, and when they are charismatic and driven, you may find yourself admiring them if their achievements match their ambition.

---

6 Burgo, J (2015) *The Narcissist You Know: Defending yourself against extreme narcissists in an all-about-me age.* New York: Touchstone Books.
7 Burgo, J (2015) '5 Types of Extreme Narcissists (and How to Deal With Them)', www.psychologytoday.com/gb/blog/shame/201509/5-types-extreme-narcissists-and-how-deal-them

- **Seductive narcissists** manipulate you by making you feel *good* about yourself. At first, they will appear to admire or even idealise you – through flattery – but their ultimate goal is to make you feel the same way about *them* so they can 'chew you up and spit you out' when they're done with you.

- **Vindictive narcissists** are the most dangerous type of all. They will try to destroy you if you pose too big a threat. You may challenge their superior status in some way you don't even recognise, and as a result, they need to prove you the ultimate loser by destroying you. They'll talk trash about you behind your back and may even try to get you fired.

These types are not clear cut – most extreme narcissists exhibit behaviours from all the types. It turns out, though, that there is one overriding mindset that prevails, regardless of the type of extreme narcissist...

'I AM A WINNER AND YOU ARE A LOSER'

The winner versus loser dynamic embodies the bully. These are highly competitive individuals who must win at all costs to support their inflated sense of self-importance. They are the winners who prove themselves superior to the losers they defeat, and they need to prove it again and again.

Bullies always need to prove that they are 'winners' in comparison to other people they view as 'losers'. This is bad news for everyone, and the more anxious extreme narcissists are about failing at their job, the more arrogant and insulting they are apt to become.

I was surprised to learn that the way my bully made me feel – like a complete and utter loser – was probably how he was feeling deep down. I realised that despite the 'brash bastard' exterior – the loud voice, the standing over people, the finger pointing, the curveballs, the backstabbing – my bully was probably denying his own shame, by projecting it (albeit unconsciously) onto those he abused every day. Desperately trying to escape from feeling defective and inferior, by making others feel like losers, bullies convince themselves that they are actually the winners.

That many bullies unconsciously hurt others' feelings was a bitter pill to swallow, as it felt like my bully knew exactly what he was doing. It explains why he could never see himself as (or admit to being) 'part of the problem'.

And bullies love to compete with the best. It was an eye opener to learn that unlike playground bullying, workplace bullying is not aimed at the weakest individual; in fact, top performers are the most likely targets. Often the most skilled person in the team, the target also tends to have better social skills, to be better liked, and to be valued for their warmth and empathy.

Because the bully views the world through a competitive lens, the successful, highly regarded target threatens to make him feel like a comparative loser. Experiencing the target as a threat, the bully will then do everything in their power to destroy both the target's reputation and their career.

Hopefully you can see how the competitive lens I am describing here is not a healthy one. Dr Craig Malkin positions narcissism as a normal pervasive human tendency: the drive to feel special.[8] As healthy competition helps us to raise the bar and perform better, so does a healthy dose of narcissism help us to pursue and realise our dreams.

---

8   Malkin, C (2015) *Rethinking Narcissism: The bad – and surprising good – about feeling special.* New York: Harper Wave.

This discovery genuinely shocked me at first. In my world, a narcissist was an arrogant and self-obsessed individual with a grandiose sense of self-importance, someone who 'knew it all' and treated others with contempt and blame. However, I've come to learn that that there is such a thing as healthy narcissism. For the first time I began to understand my own narcissism. There have been many times in my life where I've slipped into unhealthy narcissism. Narcissism exists on a spectrum of possible expressions, and at times we're all narcissistic. It therefore helps to understand what you may have in common with your bully – what are those personality traits that flip you both into unhealthy narcissism?

I won't be surprised in the slightest if you're sceptical right now and want to turn around, but please read on. Next, I am going to explore the narcissism spectrum[9] and 'common ground' concepts further.

---

9   The Narcissism Spectrum Model was developed by Dr Craig Malkin: www.drcraigmalkin.com/the-narcissism-test

THE NARCISSISM SPECTRUM

In the middle of this 'bow tie' diagram you can see a scale from 1 to 10. The desire to feel special increases as you move along from left to right on the scale.

THE NARCISSISM SPECTRUM SCALE

Credit: Dr. Craig Malkin

EXTREME ECHOISM AND NARCISSISM

Life on either side of the spectrum is a pretty scary place to be. At 0–2 on the scale, you have extreme echoism[10] – not **ego**ism, but **echo**ism – which is the complete opposite of extreme narcissism. Extreme echoists cannot stand attention or feeling special, and they literally cringe at the thought of needing anything from anybody. Extreme echoism is characterised by complete abstinence. Echoists relentlessly sacrifice their own needs to serve the needs of others and avoid the spotlight at all costs.

---

10   Davis, D (2005) 'Echo in the Darkness', *Psychoanalytic Review*, vol. 92, no. 1.

Extreme narcissists (at 8–10 on the scale) crave the spotlight. They are addicted to attention and feeling special, and like most addicts, they'll do anything to get their high. This is the danger zone; there is no empathy and all ethics and morals have been stamped out as well. The most cold, unemotional narcissists may also be psychopaths, completely devoid of sadness, anxiety, guilt, or remorse – the serial killers and fraudsters of the world. People no longer matter to them. Note: all psychopaths are narcissists, but not all narcissists are psychopaths.

SUBTLE ECHOISTS AND NARCISSISTS

Let's have a look at subtle echoists (at 2–4 on the scale) and subtle narcissists (at 6–8 on the scale). In this territory we have habit, which is good news, as habits can change; with enough self-awareness and determination someone can slide back to healthy narcissism.

Subtle echoists reflexively focus on other people's needs. It is an unconscious strategy to keep people from rejecting them. Colloquially, I refer to subtle echoists, a category I fall into from time to time, as people-pleasers. People in this range are not allergic to attention – being noticed is fine – as long as they're noticed for what they do for others. They are often productive workers and attentive listeners.

Subtle narcissists, on the other hand, are often merely bad listeners, endlessly preoccupied with how they measure up to everyone else. Unhealthy narcissists aren't always obnoxiously arrogant or openly condescending. Since winning is an easy way to feel special, they obsess over their numbers at work or compare themselves to anyone who exceeds them in looks, talent or achievement. They're constantly consulting some imaginary scoreboard in their head. We all do this from time to time, especially when the environment encourages it. These subtle narcissists often have a sense of entitlement, as though the world and everyone else owes them and should support their superior status. Entitlement can tip over into exploitation – a pattern of doing anything necessary to get ahead or stand out, including hurting other people. For people who approach 9 on the spectrum, the world largely exists for their benefit, including the people in it.

HEALTHY NARCISSISM

In the middle we have healthy narcissism. Any healthy ego will include elements of both narcissistic and echoistic trends. Narcissism, in a healthy personality, builds self-esteem and establishes boundaries regarding limits of self; similarly, echoism allows for the development of empathy and the growth of positive relationships.

Think about the most inspiring individual you know – someone you really respect and look up to. Your charismatic leader projects a self-image that inspires confidence. They see themselves as exceptional, a breed apart from ordinary people. Through the power of their conviction they persuade people to see them in the same light, and use this as a force for good, for example, treating others with kindness and respect. Holding such a self-image reflects a trust in one's strengths and abilities. 'I know who I am, and I am sure of what actions to take. I am confident I can achieve my goals.'

IN SUMMARY

Narcissism is a normal pervasive human tendency: the drive to feel special and it exists on a spectrum of possible expressions. Right at the outset, my challenge to you is to reflect on where you are on the Narcissism Spectrum Scale and to consider what behaviours you need to change in order to move into the healthy narcissism range. I hope that my story will:

- Show you that if I can do it, so can you

- Inspire you to take massive action

This is your time, dear reader.

SPOT THE BULLY PROMPTS

- A bully... threatens and humiliates
- ... destructs and derails
- Think you're the problem?
- Don't believe you're worthy?
- Can't see a way out?

TWO

THE TOXIC TRIO

'No one is born hating another person because of the color of his skin, or his background, or his religion. People must learn to hate, and if they can learn to hate, they can be taught to love, for love comes more naturally to the human heart than its opposite.'

NELSON MANDELA

It is not possible for bullies to 'destruct and derail' on their own. Much like the Fire Triangle – in which you need heat, oxygen and fuel for a fire to ignite – you need a toxic trio for a dysfunctional work relationship:

1. A bully, as defined in Chapter One – a destructive person who demeans others and derails projects.

2. A victim – this could include the person being targeted by the bully, but also the bystander, who witnesses the bullying, but does nothing. Victims and bystanders are susceptible followers. Then you also have the colluders, people who side with the bully for whatever reason. They are all victims in one way or another.

3.   An organisation's culture – a conducive work environment or 'breeding ground for bullies', typically unregulated and hostile. It allows bullying behaviours to manifest and is often a culture of fear in which people are afraid to speak up.

THE TOXIC TRIO

My thinking is inspired by the original Toxic Triangle, created by Art Padilla, Robert Hogan and Robert B Kaiser.[11]

Let's explore each component of the toxic trio in turn. We'll start with the bully.

11   Padilla, A, Hogan, R and Kaiser, RB (2007) 'The Toxic Triangle: Elements in three domains related to destructive leadership', www.researchgate.net/figure/The-toxic-triangle-elements-in-three-domains-related-to-destructive-leadership_fig1_222521379

THE BULLY: WHAT ARE THE SIGNS?

Recognising a bully is easier said than done. In Chapter One we looked at the characteristics of bullies in the context of narcissism. Bullies are often highly charismatic and capable individuals in positions of power. They carefully navigate and shrewdly circumvent organisational constructs. These are the three crucial signs that you're dealing with a bully:

1. Can't establish and maintain healthy, trusted long-term relationships, sees people as objects, not as people

2. Arrogant and lacks self-awareness – 'I am the bee's knees and can do nothing wrong'

3. Rigid, inflexible, unable to learn – 'It's my way or the highway'

Bullies often sneak up on us when our guard is down. We don't expect outright rudeness or dishonesty at work, so we tend to doubt the shocking behaviour when we encounter it: 'Surely he didn't just humiliate me in front of everyone?' Somehow, we convince ourselves it didn't really happen. Worse, we blame ourselves. We explain away our colleague's bad behaviour. We hope tomorrow will be better.

We all get days when we are feeling tired, stressed and irritable; days when we are more likely to 'lose our cool' and say something we regret later. These 'blips' can be repaired if we apologise and acknowledge our mistakes. Most of us can do this after we've calmed down. Real bullies can't say sorry, or if they do they end up repeating the same behaviour and this becomes a vicious cycle of 'lash out and apologise'. After a while, the apologies no longer mean anything. Saying sorry without genuine regret is manipulation.

When you're keeping company with a bully, the put-downs and finger pointing increase over time and become a pattern. Bullies use arrogance and self-importance to force people into supporting roles, and to make others feel inferior. Although this may not be obvious, bullies actually need the people they bully – for their daily narcissistic 'fix', to feel better about themselves and to boost their fragile self-esteem. For a bully to be victorious, someone else must always lose – no matter what.

SETTING BOUNDARIES

The aim here is to recognise bullying behaviour early on and do something about it. If you don't set boundaries early, and more importantly keep those boundaries, the behaviour will persist, escalate and become normalised. Setting boundaries is one of the hardest things to do. Bullies are master manipulators and they mess with people's heads. It is definitely one of their most destructive traits.

I regret that I allowed my bully to repeatedly overstep the line I drew early on. However, with the benefit of hindsight I know that he was a special case and that I had no chance of stopping him. After I desperately and unsuccessfully presented my case to HR, I had no choice but to walk away. If you've tried everything and your actions are getting you nowhere, you have some legal options available to you; I explore these in Chapter Eight.

Some of the most common bullying behaviours to look out for are:

- Verbal abuse eg shouting, humiliating, swearing

- Work sabotage eg undermining, interference, shifting goals

- Extreme criticism eg hurling insults and demoralising comments

- Abuse of power eg blaming others, stealing credit, denying promotions
- Intimidation eg threatening to demote or fire, refusing requests for time off
- Isolation (or exclusion) eg punishing non-delivery, spreading rumours
- Inconsistent, unfair treatment eg 'different strokes for different folks'

OVERT AND COVERT BULLIES

Unlike the typical 'brash bastard' exterior of the overt bully, covert bullies are more like snakes in suits: less 'in your face' but extremely poisonous. They will say what you want to hear and bite you in the back when you least expect it. What you see is definitely not what you get. It's therefore important to figure out who you can and cannot trust, without being paranoid, of course. Again, this is not easy.

If you are an empath, like me, it will be in your nature to look for the good in others. We tend to give people the benefit of the doubt. We justify the toxic behaviours listed above. We aim to please others. Bullies can smell us a mile away and will exploit this every time. After a recent encounter with a covert bully I told Heinie, my husband, 'I think I am a bully magnet.'

Of course, I know this is not true, but I do believe that some people are more prone to becoming targets. Be careful who you trust and allow to influence you. Apply a healthy dose of scepticism. Trust has to be earned.

THE VICTIM: RECOGNISE YOUR OWN BEHAVIOURS

During my exit process, I felt scared, lonely and tired, and at the mercy of my bully and the organisational constructs surrounding me. It felt like a scene from a horror movie. The days went by in a haze and I couldn't imagine this happening to anyone else. Shortly after I left, I confided in three people, all highly successful senior executives. I honestly didn't expect to hear another three horror stories, but they all had one. In the months that followed, as I regained perspective and got my life back on track, I realised that workplace bullying is the silent epidemic of the twenty-first century business landscape.

I became obsessed with why the vast majority of targets either just 'suck it up' or leave quietly, and analysed my own reasons.

You don't believe that the organisation is going to do anything to help you. You explain away the bully's shocking behaviour. You worry about finding another job, and about the people who will be left behind. In the process, you become so mentally and physically exhausted that you cannot think straight anymore. You leave quietly, with your reputation intact.

What if I said to you that a bully can only take your power if you give it to him? Let that sink in for a moment: a bully can only take your power if you give it to him.

It's true. It's OK if you are struggling to comprehend this right now. If you are in a situation at work where someone is making your life miserable, you probably feel that you're at their mercy. They are probably someone in a position of power – typically the boss or one of the boss's cronies.

That's OK, but please recognise your own behaviour. What is holding you back? Low self-esteem? Fear? Self-limiting beliefs and excuses? In Chapter Six I further explain how the mind works, and how to stay in your power zone.

It's sad to see how many targets blame themselves, even years after their experience of being bullied. They grapple with questions such as: why did I allow someone to bully me? Was I imagining it? Is this just the way things are in the corporate world, that only the fittest and most ruthless will survive? Maybe I just wasn't good enough. Even long after our experience, we still try to justify the bully's behaviour.

If you are currently in a bullying situation – or you think you might be – how do you respond?

My own research and experience show that the most common responses are to keep quiet or to become defensive. Few people challenge the bully's behaviour. When you challenge or become defensive it is like throwing fuel on the fire. The bully cannot and will not admit that their behaviour is inappropriate. That would be the same as saying, 'I am a loser.' Real bullies cannot see how they are part of the problem.

The downside of this reaction is that by 'sucking it up' we normalise the bully's behaviour. They think it's OK to treat others with contempt and disrespect. It is never OK. As targets, we have to try to set and keep boundaries, escalate if necessary, and if that doesn't work, walk away. In Chapter Three, I encourage you to take action, and provide options to help you figure out the right course of action.

Whatever you decide to do, please promise me that you will stay true to yourself. Don't try to change who you are because someone else is threatened by your existence.

Also, know this: it is *not* your responsibility to deal with a bully. It's the organisation's legal and moral responsibility to stamp out bullying behaviour, to protect the people who work there.

Sadly, organisations are failing. Too many people feel unsafe asking for help. Why?

WORKPLACE CULTURE: HELPING OR HINDERING?

Workplace culture, simply defined as 'the way we do things around here', either helps or hinders workplace bullies in destructing and derailing projects and people. A staggering 90% of my survey respondents said that their organisation's culture made it easier for the bully.

Not only is bullying a silent epidemic, it's also a silent killer.

AMNESTY INTERNATIONAL CASE STUDY

I was shaken to the core when I read a report[12] into the workplace culture of Amnesty International, a leading human rights nongovernmental organisation (NGO), and the results of a review into staff wellbeing following the suicides of two of its workers. Gaëtan Mootoo made it clear in his suicide note that work pressures, among other things, were major factors in his decision to end his life.

The report found that despite workers' routine exposure to suffering, abuse and trauma, the most significant contributor to wellbeing issues were an adversarial workplace culture, failures in management and HR department failures.

Overall, the Amnesty report describes a 'toxic' working environment, with widespread bullying, public humiliation, discrimination and other abuses of power; it also found a dangerous 'us versus them' dynamic, and a severe lack of trust in managers.

---

12   Amnesty International (2019) 'Amnesty International Staff Wellbeing Review', www.amnesty.org/download/Documents/ORG6097632019ENGLISH.PDF

The themes from the Amnesty report chime with my own experiences and what others have told me, particularly in relation to HR failures. According to my research study, more than half of survey respondents and interviewees didn't inform HR about bullying either because they feared retribution or because they didn't trust HR to have their best interests at heart. A quarter said HR did nothing despite requests for support. Only 10% said HR resolved or attempted to resolve the situation positively, completely or partially. The rest said that HR intervened too late or that they didn't know. HR departments need to raise their game.

ELIMINATING THE 'US VERSUS THEM' CULTURAL DYNAMIC

As in the Amnesty International report, my research pointed to a widespread 'us versus them' cultural dynamic in organisations and a troubling lack of trust in managers. This feeling is essentially the 'fight' in the 'fight or flight' response that comprises the human reaction to a threat of survival. It is highly stressful and typically results in a destructive tendency on both sides to blame and villainise the 'other' rather than acknowledge one's own part in any conflict.

So how does this dynamic play out?

Managers typically abuse their positions of power by making idle threats and avoiding or dismissing complaints of unfair processes or bullying. Workers then villainise managers as privileged, out of touch, incompetent and callous. Both sides are clearly pushing back at each other and (essentially) pushing each other away. Here are some examples of this dynamic:

'Us' (managers)	'Them' (workers)
■ Dismiss concerns of long-serving workers as the gripes of 'old timers'	■ Believe incompetent managers should be fired
■ Dismiss requests for assistance or accommodations arising from 'an entitlement culture'	■ Accuse management teams of not getting along
■ Suggest that unhappy workers can 'take it or leave it'	■ Believe managers lack transparency and are poor communicators
	■ Accuse managers of saying one thing, then doing something completely different

For organisations to function optimally, everyone – managers and workers – should take personal responsibility for overcoming this 'us versus them' dynamic. This starts with senior leaders. In Chapter Eight I provide best practice guidance on how to have difficult conversations and build trusted relationships.

At this point, although I sincerely hope it's not the case, you may still wonder: why go through the trouble?

The most important reason is because it is the right thing to do. If you are a leader that is serious about your organisation's bottom line, and the mental and physical health of your people, it's time to stop looking the other way. Don't become complicit.

TOXIC CULTURES ARE COSTLY

The financial and emotional cost directly attributable to toxic cultures is staggering. In reality it's usually the highest performers, the top talent, who quit. Here is a rough indication of the financial costs of replacing your best people, according to research by Dr Mitchell Kusy:

- For mid-level employees it's upwards of 150% of annual salary
- For high-level, specialised employees, costs can ramp up to 400% of annual salary[13]

A recent article in the *Financial Times*, 'The Trillion-dollar Taboo: Why it's time to stop ignoring mental health at work', further highlights how workplace stress is costing businesses dearly.[14]

The number of people who revealed to me that they had experienced suicidal thoughts, including a couple of failed suicide attempts, deeply shocked me. I remember when the thought of walking in front of a bus briefly entered my mind; it scared the living daylights out of me and I promised myself to never go there again. I can't help but wonder what might have happened if my mental health wasn't strong enough at the time.

This a real and serious problem. A cultural change is needed to prevent workplace bullying from happening in the first place. Why don't organisations protect the mental and physical health of their human capital, the most valuable assets?

It's time to wake up and smell the coffee. Stop turning a blind eye. Don't wait until it's too late.

---

13 Kusy, M (2017) *Why I Don't Work Here Anymore: A leader's guide to offset the financial and emotional costs of toxic employees.* Boca Raton: Productivity Press.

14 Raptopoulos, L and Fontanella-Khan, J (2019) 'The Trillion-dollar Taboo: Why it's time to stop ignoring mental health at work', *Financial Times*, 11 July, www.ft.com/content/1e8293f4-a1db-11e9-974c-ad1c6ab5efd1

HOW IS BEING BULLIED PREVENTING YOU FROM BEING HIGH PERFORMING?

My bullying experience left me feeling empty, without purpose and exhausted. Feeling as though I was lacking direction and spiralling out of control was completely out of character, and I was tired of it. Something had to change. I had to get my life back on the successful path I had previously been travelling on, a path full of meaning and fulfilment. The three steps I took were to:

1. GET HONEST about my situation and face it	Chapter Three: Take Action
2. GET CLEAR about my purpose and decide what I wanted to do with my life	Chapter Four: Find Your Purpose Chapter Five: Set And Achieve Your Goals
3. GET HELP and access the support required to get me there	Chapter Six: Win The Inner Game Chapter Seven: Win The Outer Game Chapter Eight: ROAR! Communicate With Impact And Influence

IN SUMMARY

We weather storms every day – that is just life. We're either approaching a storm, in a storm or coming out of one. If you don't value yourself – practising healthy narcissism – and give yourself permission to be a high performer, you are going to get sucked in by the storm, and there is a good chance that it will destroy you in the process. The benefit of a high performance lifestyle is that it equips you with the mental, physical and emotional tools and techniques to weather these storms. The rest of my book is all about speaking up, ie calling out unacceptable behaviour, and becoming a high performer living your best life.

I hope you're excited to go on this journey with me.

GET HONEST PROMPTS

- Does life suck right now?
- Are you ready to face the storm?
- Can you face it alone?
  - Think so... Chart your next move
  - No way... Ask for help

THREE

TAKE ACTION

'Not everything that is faced can be changed, but nothing can be changed until it is faced'

JAMES BALDWIN

If you are a victim or a witness of workplace bullying – if your workplace is toxic and a breeding ground for bullying behaviour (overt or covert) – this chapter is going to be a tough read for you. You will have to face some truths.

Expect it to evoke a lot of emotions, including guilt, anger, fear, sadness, worry and shame. Allow yourself to feel these emotions and realise that the only way you can change the status quo is to be honest with yourself.

My aim in this chapter is to encourage you to evaluate your current situation; to hold a mirror up and to take action if you don't like what you see. To illustrate, I share the stories of Ben, Mark and Sarah – all high performers – and although I am not using their real names, their stories are 100% real.

I also share with you the practical tips and strategies that helped me to take back my power, find the courage to speak up and to deal with difficult conversations more effectively.

IT'S EASIER SAID THAN DONE

If you're working for a bully, you're probably saying this right now. I understand. These situations are complex. How can you be sure you are being bullied, let alone find the courage to speak up?

BEN'S STORY

Ben, a senior executive in a large global consulting firm, was running a team of 50 people. Times were good and the business was growing strongly.

Then a new boss started. He arrived with a reputation for getting rid of anyone who would not conform to his ways of working. He introduced lots of his own ideas and initiatives which he expected the staff to implement without question and without impacting anything else.

Any attempts to discuss these initiatives were met with a stiff rebuke about inefficient working practices and an implied threat that people's jobs were at risk. It quickly became clear that the new boss was aloof and standoffish, saw employees as production units rather than people, and had no empathy with anyone except his own superiors.

A climate of fear began to fester as impossible deadlines loomed. The previously enthusiastic team turned into a group of individuals who believed they were facing a no-win situation. Some were placed on 'make or break' performance improvement programmes. In Ben's own words:

'Personally, I was put under a great deal of pressure. This affected my professional demeanour and home life. I found myself displaying all the signs of stress: sleeping badly, comfort eating, neglecting my friends and relations, and working far too many long hours. Even when I was off work, the thought of having to return and attempt to meet impossible deadlines made me deeply unhappy.

'I approached my boss on a number of occasions, but to no avail; there was only criticism – no help and no support. Eventually, major deadlines were missed as the squeeze on available resources took its toll. I was told that I had "let him down" as I failed to administer my team to meet all his demands. I would therefore be removed from the role and a new intermediate boss brought in above me.

'Producing data to demonstrate how I had managed with limited resources cut no ice. Furthermore, as my boss was a partner in the organisation, (a) there was no one I could approach to plead my case and (b) I feared for my job should I contact HR and raise a complaint. After all, I had already seen him dispose of a number of people across the wider business who had "let him down".

'The outcome for me was humiliation and effective demotion. If I was concerned for my job before, I was paranoid about it now and feared to say or do anything which would mark me as a troublemaker. Consequently, my work, personal life and health suffered even more. I was struggling so badly I went to counselling to address my issues.'

Does this sound familiar? It does to me. After countless failed attempts to make my bully see that he was part of the problem, and how his impossible demands and constant put-downs damaged team morale and negatively impacted our ability to deliver, he nearly destroyed me.

I don't want the same to happen to you. I want you to speak up before the situation gets out of hand, or so bad that it affects your health and relationships. First, let's have a look at some of the common pitfalls to avoid.

DEALING WITH A BULLY: COMMON PITFALLS

There is disturbingly little research on how to cope with workplace bullies. My research shows that people are ill equipped. This is how people say they typically respond:

1. Keep quiet
2. Get defensive
3. Confront the bully

How do you normally respond?

Unfortunately, my research tells a depressing story. At one point, I even caught myself asking: 'Can people really be trained to better manage confrontations with a bully? Perhaps it won't make a blind bit of difference.'

Sadly, many survey respondents said that their responses to bullying behaviour didn't work. If fact, less than 5% of respondents reported improved behaviour on the part of the bully as a result of their challenge. Things either stayed the same, got worse or the bully blamed the victim.

To help put things into context, let's briefly pause to draw out another key element from my research – the way people said they felt when being bullied.

PLEASE DESCRIBE THE EMOTIONS YOU FELT WHEN BULLIED

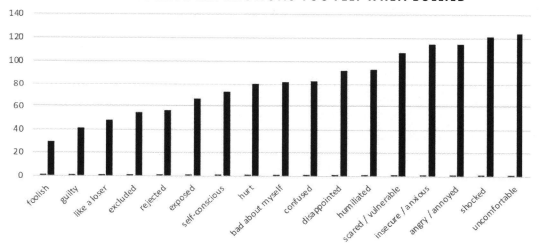

The data shows that people's reactions result from two mindsets:

- 'I'm not OK': I'm uncomfortable dealing with the bully, I don't feel I have the necessary skills, I feel unable to cope, so I'll just keep quiet.

- 'You're not OK': You never listen, you are wrong, you won't win this one, so I'll get defensive or confront you.

As a liberating leadership and high performance coach, I do a lot of work with individuals and teams around mindset, and the importance of approaching interactions with an 'I'm OK, you're OK' mindset. It is derived from transactional analysis as a method for solving problems – in this case, difficult relationships. Before any interaction, it is important that you feel good about yourself ('I'm OK'), and that you also have positive regard for the other person ('you're OK'), and to hold on to this mindset when the going gets tough.

Unfortunately, we often believe that we are the problem and that the bully is right, probably because they are in a position of power and abusing that power, so an 'I'm not OK, you're OK' mindset presides. We are biased towards justifying the bully's behaviour.

COPING STRATEGIES

#1: HAVE AN 'I'M OK, YOU'RE OK' MINDSET

I'll cover mindset further in Chapter Six, but I wanted to make you aware now that your mindset – what you think and feel about yourself and others – ultimately determines how you communicate and handle conflict. Our thoughts (conscious and unconscious) become our feelings and ultimately guide what we say and do.

#2: HOLD ON TO YOUR POWER

It's not just the bully doing everything in their power to be the winner and make you out to be the loser (remember the winner versus loser dynamic). The actions of your inner bully – your self-limiting beliefs and fears – mean that you are playing right into the bully's hands, essentially handing them your power on a silver platter.

#3: BLOCK THE (EMOTIONAL HOT POTATO) PASS

Did you know that the bully is making you feel the same way they feel deep inside, although they will rarely admit it?

People on the far right of the narcissism spectrum (see Chapter One) love playing 'emotional hot potato' – it's a way of dealing with their own inner struggles. It is a more insidious form of projection in which people deny their own feelings by claiming they belong to someone else. In emotional hot potato, people don't simply confuse their own feelings with someone else's; they actually coerce you into experiencing the emotions they're trying to ignore in the first place.

If you're feeling helpless or overwhelmed after an interaction with anyone at work, you may well be the target of an attempted hot potato pass. You'll need to block it, although it's hard not to get sucked in by the bully's drama – they go out of their way to provoke. I often refer to energy vampires who try everything in their power to suck the lifeblood out of you. Remember, they can only do it if you allow them to.

For the remaining three strategies, we'll go back to the three ways survey participants said they typically responded, and explore a different strategy for each.

#4: DON'T KEEP QUIET

Keeping quiet is the natural response. You've been criticised or belittled but you say nothing and do nothing. You take the abuse because you want to keep the peace. Worse, you justify the bully's behaviour. Does this sound familiar? Put your hand up and see what might happen.

MARK'S STORY

'One senior manager (C-level) would say to people in meetings, "You're fired," if they said something he didn't like. He thought it was funny, but it clearly reminded everyone of the power dynamic. It made everyone feel uncomfortable; we all lost respect for the bully (I know because we discussed it). However, no one said anything.

'Another senior manager (also C-level) had a habit of referring to people as "lettuce leaves" behind their backs – a clear indication that he didn't rate them. Again, we all kept quiet.

'These managers used their positions of authority to intimidate us. We knew that questioning their thinking would be to the detriment of our careers, so we said nothing – even if we knew they were wrong. We just accepted it as the way things were. Not only did I lose respect for these managers, I also lost respect for myself, as I knew that I wasn't being authentic. I didn't speak up. I suspect that the colleagues who witnessed these situations also lost respect for me, as they knew I chickened out.

'There was also a general loss of faith in the espoused values of the organisation – it turned out that all the propaganda about treating people fairly and with respect was just corporate "mumbo jumbo".

'Many of the culprits went on to have very successful careers. It's not as if the managers of these people didn't know what was going on. They were well aware of who the bullies were, but chose to turn a blind eye, as they (supposedly) got results.'

Mark's story highlights some of the repercussions of not speaking up; it often creates more problems than it solves. Losing respect for yourself and others is bad news. Again, it's easier said than done.

Have you tried going against the big boss? The last time I did, it cost me my job. At least I did the right thing and left with my reputation intact.

But here's the rub: by doing nothing, we inadvertently signal to the bully that their behaviour is acceptable. Every time they get away with it, it becomes more and more normalised and embedded in the cultural norms – 'the way we do things around here'.

My bully would make snarky comments behind people's backs if they kept quiet. 'Picture, but no sound,' he would growl in his usual condescending tone, comparing them to a muted television. I never said anything, just sheepishly laughed it off, and quietly hated myself for it.

About six months before I left, I called a friend after enduring another day from hell. An experienced team member was struggling to deliver a project. The boss wanted her out, but I pushed back. He raised his voice, told me that I had better fix this, that he was sick and tired of doing my job for me, and said that I would be penalised for my team member's 'failures'. There was of course no mention of some shocking decisions on his part that had got us to this point in the first place. I did nothing. My friend told me that the next time he raised he voice, I should put my hand up in front of me and say, 'Stop. I won't allow you to speak to me like that.' But by then it was too late for me; I'd allowed him to get away with it for too long. Leaving was my only option.

#5: DON'T GET DEFENSIVE

Although it feels personal, it's not.

> *'Their response was I am too sensitive. That it was the corporate culture and I needed to develop a thicker skin. Some of the responses I can't repeat because it's too painful.'*

Does this comment from a survey respondent sound familiar?

Getting defensive was the primary tactic I used against my bully. Little did I realise just how much I played right into his hands and how much he enjoyed making me feel the way he so desperately didn't want to feel himself.

Why do we get defensive? It's to defend ourselves against certain truths. We're often in denial, and struggle to cope with the negative perceptions of others. We want others to see us the way we see ourselves. When they don't, we feel insecure and respond impulsively.

SARAH'S STORY

Sarah, a director in a global research firm, was responsible for delivery across an entire project portfolio. A few projects had been in trouble, and one in particular was failing. During their weekly management team meeting – with six others present – Sarah was in the middle of updating her boss on the status of this particular project when he suddenly started lashing out, criticising the team left, right and centre. He expressed his disappointment, how he was tired of all the excuses, how people were incapable of doing the job, how they were all failing.

Sarah was frustrated and didn't know what to do any more. A lot of the problems were related to poor decisions made by her boss, but of course he was blaming everyone else. When Sarah defended her position, he accused her of having a 'hissy fit', and when she denied this, he silenced her, turning to start a new conversation with someone else.

At that point Sarah felt anxious and close to tears. She excused herself from the meeting to get some water. When she returned to the meeting room he carried on as if nothing had happened. After the meeting Sarah sent her colleague a message to ask what he thought of their boss's behaviour at the meeting. The colleague never replied.

#6: DON'T FIGHT THE BULLY

Be careful how you confront the bully. In the early days, when I was still oblivious to being bullied, I challenged my bully a lot. As his deputy, I was pulled into his office like clockwork every morning. Sometimes he was in good spirits and acting like my 'best friend', but most days he had a problem with something or someone that he expected me sort out.

What I didn't realise at the time is that I had become his drug. He was addicted to controlling me and our daily interactions gave him his regular narcissistic 'fix'.

One morning, I was accused of creating a flexible working culture, which was an outright lie. He expected staff to be in the office at 9am, five days a week. He fostered an illusion that once you proved you were capable of delivering you would be trusted to work from home. Of course, this never happened as no one was ever allowed to prove themselves trustworthy enough. It was a vicious cycle.

I was furious and deeply hurt by his false accusations. I decided to write him a letter, telling him that his behaviour was unacceptable and unprofessional.

After reading the letter he was livid and summoned me to his office where I spent over two hours enduring insult after insult. I was reminded over and over just how much I was wasting his precious time. At one point during the meeting he even compared our relationship to a 'marriage in trouble'. Utterly confused, I left the meeting with my tail between my legs. Things got better, but only for a short while.

Have you ever written to someone to complain about their behaviour? What was their reaction?

I thought my assertive tactic would work. I had clearly said, 'Your behaviour is unprofessional, unacceptable and makes me feel unappreciated. I don't take kindly to being falsely accused.' Now I know that bullies cannot absorb honest, accurate feedback. They're extreme narcissists, after all, so they just get angrier and more aggressive. As I did, you are likely to face a verbal lashing if you try this tactic.

Anger makes narcissists of all of us. By venting my anger and frustration directly at my bully, I was fighting narcissism with narcissism. I became defensive because his constant criticism felt an assault on my self-esteem. We're only human and, no matter how caring our nature, most of us will choose either a fight, flight or freeze survival response when under attack. We become less compassionate as we defend ourselves. Change becomes impossible.

HIGH PERFORMANCE COPING STRATEGIES

As well as the earlier coping strategies, there are three high performance strategies that will help you to tame your bully in the long run:

1.   Win the inner game.

2.   Win the outer game.

3.   ROAR! Communicate with impact and influence.

I call these my three life lessons. By now you know that each life lesson forms a chapter in my book. In this chapter, I briefly introduce some of the pertinent concepts around how to cope better with difficult situations. We'll explore the psychology and physiology behind these concepts further in the remaining chapters.

#1: Win the inner game

Your ability to 'hold your nerve' depends largely on your ability to control your own emotions and approach every interaction with the right mindset and attitude. It's also important to have empathy.

Some bullies are so self-absorbed, socially tone deaf and outright dangerous that it may feel like a superhuman challenge to empathise with a bully. They cause havoc in our lives and the greater their power and influence the more they affect how you feel about yourself.

Rise above it, block the pass. It's hard, I know, but it's important that you try. Remember the following:

- Extreme narcissists are always in flight from pain. Deep down they are insecure, perhaps even ashamed, as a result of suffering trauma in their past, most likely as a child.

- We saw in Chapter One that 'once a narcissist, always a narcissist' doesn't necessarily hold true. Recent studies indicate that if narcissists in the habit range – around 7–8 on the spectrum – are approached in a gentler way, many seem to soften emotionally.[15] It's worth a try.

'I'm OK, you're OK': Remember that it's their *behaviour* that is not OK, not the actual person themselves. It is vital that you enter any difficult situation, however hard it may be, with two underlying attitudes:

---

15   Malkin, C (2015) *Rethinking Narcissism: The bad – and surprising good – about feeling special.* New York: Harper Wave.

- **Positive regard:** This means having compassion and respect for the other person as an individual and positive belief in them as a person. Irrespective of the behaviour they are currently displaying, you see the good in them and view them as fundamentally a good, decent human being.

- **Genuineness:** This means you are able to express your own feelings and tell the truth about your reactions to the other person's behaviour. It means being direct, open and honest with them, and not shying away from a difficult conversation.

#2: Win the outer game

This is all about energy management and appearances, showing up every day as the best version of you and staying above it all. Don't get sucked into other people's drama and negativity. I remember being exhausted and wiped out. I had no energy left to spend quality time with myself and the people who really mattered. My bullying boss became my energy vampire.

Negative people are usually committed to being negative. The more you push them to be anything else, the more they will push back. Therefore, don't put your energy into negative people or your life will be negative. Keep your focus on what is good, and you will see more good. It will grow, just like a muscle does with exercise.

Good energy management is all about nutrition, exercise, de-stressing and refuelling your mind and body; this is vitally important to keep you mentally and physically strong. It seems so simple, but how many of us are actually getting these basics right?

It's particularly hard to stay cool, calm and collected when you're dealing with a bully and you feel like you're fighting battles every day. How do you keep a poker face if your heart is racing and you want to explode inside?

You breathe. Keep calm and carry on.

You need your whole self, your spirit, your emotions, your mental strength, and your physical wellbeing to be aligned and working together. I realise there is no magic pill but if you believe you can overcome the problem, you're already halfway there.

#3: ROAR! Communicate with impact and influence

As we've seen, falling silent is not the answer; neither is getting defensive or confronting the bully in a way that gets his back up. You have to find your own unique ROAR! Remember, your goal is to manage the bully, not to foster closeness.

Here are my top ten tips for managing a bully:

1. Set goals – what would indicate that the situation is improving for you?
2. Release your fears – don't let them sabotage your growth and success
3. Empower yourself – give yourself permission to speak up
4. Have empathy – 'I'm OK, you're OK'
5. Protect yourself – set clear boundaries and document everything
6. Resist the urge to retaliate – stay cool, calm and collected
7. Remain focused on the task – tie it to common goals and workplace success
8. Block the pass – try to avoid damage to your self-esteem

9.   Catch good behaviour – illustrate the benefits of collaboration

10. Use your power – develop the inner strength and confidence to ROAR!

My three life lessons, including my top ten tips above, form the basis of how I strive to live my life. The rest of this book will provide more guidance on the knowledge, skills and habits you'll need to tame your bully and to live your best life.

IN SUMMARY

I hope that the stories in this chapter will show you that doing nothing is not an option. It creates more problems in the long run, and the reality is that people rarely change. Be realistic; you may not be able to smooth things over with your bully. Don't hold on to the false hope that they will change once you've proved yourself worthy. You are worthy – full stop – and deserve to be treated with respect. Remember, it's your employer's legal and moral responsibility to protect you.

If you've tried everything and your actions are getting nowhere, you have legal options available to you. I'll tell you more about these in Chapter Eight, but first I want you to read the rest of the book. I passionately believe – and know from decades of experience – that the office bully can be tamed.

It starts with taming our inner bully.

TAME THE INNER BULLY PROMPTS

- I am not the problem
- I am enough
- It's not personal
- I deserve to be treated with respect
- Others deserve my respect as well

FOUR

FIND YOUR PURPOSE

'Isn't it amazing how the biggest hurdles that leave us feeling so damaged ultimately shape our career and outcome, giving our lives an entirely new meaning?!'

AMY DAVIES

When Amy, the CEO of First 30 Inc. and author of *A Spark in the Dark*, said this to me a couple of months ago it made so much sense. However, a couple of years ago I would have struggled to hear it, even though I knew deep down it was true. By now you know that my experience had left me feeling empty and without purpose. My life was spiralling out of control. I was tired of it. I knew that I had to get my life back on the successful path I had been travelling on; a path full of joy, meaning and fulfilment. I felt lost and couldn't see a way out.

If you are currently in a bullying situation, I suspect that 'purpose' is the last thing on your mind. You probably feel stuck too. I totally get that – I spent years in denial. However, don't make the same mistakes I made. Don't allow your bully to grind you down to the point where you lose all sense of purpose and self. You owe it to yourself to:

- **Get honest** about your situation and face it, as discussed in the previous chapter.

- **Get clear** about your purpose and decide what you want your life to look like, as I'll discuss in this chapter.

- **Get help** and access the support required to get you there, as I'll share in the remaining chapters of this book.

CLARITY ABOUT YOUR PURPOSE

It's ironic that my bully introduced me to the concept of high performance when we first started working together. He prided himself on a track record of building high-performing teams and expected the same of me. About a year in, the team was in turmoil, and I was desperate to help them and transform us into a high-performing team. That's what he said he wanted, and I was determined to prove myself. I was blinded by my own ambition.

One evening I noticed an advertisement on Facebook for a High Performance Master's Programme. It was an advanced online training and personal development coaching course with Brendon Burchard. I signed up straight away. Little did I know at the time that this decision would literally transform my own life too, and that I would also one day call myself a Certified High Performance Coach (CHPC).

I discovered that high performance meant different things to different people. It certainly wasn't what I was led to believe initially – remember the 'I am a winner and you are a loser' dynamic from Chapter Two? Those highly competitive individuals who must win at all costs to support their inflated sense of self-importance; the winners who prove themselves superior to the losers they defeat; the need to prove it again and again. I was intrigued to learn about the 'toxic high performer', as I don't believe these words belong together in the same sentence.

This is what high performance means to me:

> *Reaching heightened levels of personal and professional success consistently over the long term – doing what you love – while maintaining positive relationships and personal wellbeing.*

Yes, it is possible to be successful, happy and healthy. In fact, it is essential. You cannot otherwise sustain success over long periods of time. The rat race will catch up with you sooner or later.

Not too long ago, this seemed completely unattainable to me. I didn't feel like a high performer at all. Somehow, despite feeling lost, I found the inner strength and courage to fight back. I knew I had more to offer. I had to reignite my purpose, which I knew was to help people grow, be successful, and be happy.

That's why I want to assure you that no matter how challenging your current situation is, you can and will get through this.

WHAT IS IT GOING TO TAKE?

My book shines a light on how I strive to live my life as a high performer. I've developed a model for high performance which is based on a process I've been using all my life to work through tough situations and get my life back on track. When I was younger, I used this exact same process – only it was largely unconscious and more intuitive – in an 'I can wing it' kind of way. Today, as a high performer, I am a lot more intentional in how I approach my life's work. For every goal I set, I need a game plan, structure and consistency. I need to see tangible progress every day. Here is my model for living your best life – and the rest of my book – in a nutshell.

INTRODUCING MY 'YOUR BEST LIFE' MODEL

YOUR BEST LIFE MODEL

Let's break the model down.

- This chapter, *find your purpose*, covers Steps 1 and 2.
    - Step 1: Purpose – who are you today, who do you want to become and why?
    - Step 2: Momentum – which you'll get from belief in yourself, making a decision and taking massive action.
- *Make your best life a reality* – this will be covered in Chapter Five. It includes everything you need to set and achieve your goals, no matter what.
    - Step 3: Game plan – what you need to do by when. You've got to have strategies and tactics, which include realistic timelines of when you're going to get it done by.
    - Step 4: Creativity – how specifically are you going to do it? You also need the tools, resources and systems to deliver.
    - Step 5: Ability – you've got to acquire the necessary knowledge, skills and habits. I put this one last because you have to trust in your ability to figure things out. I usually set goals that I have no idea at first how I am going to deliver; for example, writing this book.

My three life lessons (indicated at the bottom of the model in the figure above) will set you apart from the pack. To me, this is what high performance is about.

- *Win the inner game* (Chapter Six) covers psychology and neuroscience – how the brain works and how to prime your mindset for success. Mastering goal achievement begins with mastering the inner game.
- *Win the outer game* (Chapter Seven) covers the physiology – generating and reserving energy to play at the pro level. This means training like an

athlete and fuelling your body for success. If you master this, everything else you dream of will available to you.

- *ROAR!* (Chapter Eight) covers how to communicate with impact and influence. ROAR is my four-step process for dealing effectively with difficult conversations.

YOUR BEST LIFE: STEPS 1 AND 2

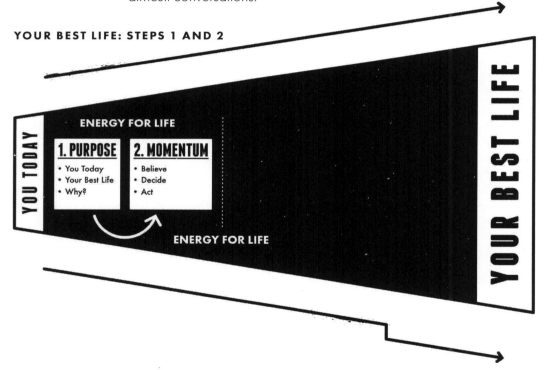

This is the first component of my model. It's all about finding your purpose and designing your best life. Let's get started on Step 1.

STEP 1: FIND (OR REIGNITE) YOUR PURPOSE

If you are currently in an abusive work relationship then your confidence is probably knocked daily and you're not feeling like a high performer. In fact, one senior manager told me:

> 'I've just read your article on workplace culture and felt compelled to get in touch. That article could have been written about me. I've always been considered a high performer but in July last year that all changed. The perpetrator was my line manager and the toxic culture he created has almost destroyed me. Fortunately, there were other victims and the HR department took our complaints seriously. In the New Year he left the organisation but the after effects linger. I am no longer the happy, confident leader I once was.'

My wish for you is that you start being honest with yourself and face your situation; that you dream big and gain clarity about who you are and what you want to achieve in life. Find the courage to do whatever it takes to make your dreams a reality. Become obsessed. Don't let fear, self-doubt and self-limiting beliefs hold you back. You are wasting your valuable life by allowing fear to control you. You've got to start holding your life in the highest regard when you ask yourself: 'Is what I am trading my life for worth it?'

If your situation at work is unbearable due to a toxic leader or environment, perhaps it's time to walk away. Maybe it's time to face your biggest fear. For how long are you prepared to be a punchbag? How much longer are you going to allow your health and relationships to suffer? Until it's too late? Don't do it to yourself.

Find your 'thing', then pursue it relentlessly.

Start by doing the exercise below.

DESIGN YOUR BEST LIFE: EXERCISE

Pretend it is a year from now: You're looking back. It's been the best year of your life.

- What kind of impact are you having on other people?
- What significance do you have?
- How much money are you making?
- What is your contribution?

Ask yourself: what do you want to change your life for? Don't ask yourself if you are worthy of the goals and the vision you have for your life, ask if the vision and the goals are worthy of your life.

Remember, you've got to start holding your life in the highest regard when you ask yourself, 'Is what I am trading my life for worth it?' Let me ask you four questions:

- Where are you today?
- Where do you want to go?
- Why do you want it?
- How are you going to get there?

Let's dig deeper into each one.

WHERE ARE YOU TODAY?

What is going on in your life right now? All change starts with one thing: being honest with yourself. I realised that I was unhappy in so many areas of my life:

- My relationships were suffering.

- My health was deteriorating.

- I worried about money and providing for my family.

- I felt unwelcome; I didn't think that I was going to survive in the industry.

- I felt dead inside – I rarely felt fun or joy.

Does this sound familiar?

Now I am in a completely different place. I left my job, started my own business, doubled my income, got into the best shape of my life (more about this in Chapter Seven) and realised exactly who I am and what I want to achieve. This was only possible because I held the mirror up and re-evaluated my life with complete honesty.

It's time to be honest with yourself. If absolutely everything was perfect, you probably wouldn't be reading this right now. Where are you today?

- Are you in a job that you hate? Or in a job you like but with a toxic individual or culture that is making your life hell?

- Are you an entrepreneur in your soul, but scared to start the business?

- Are you crushing it financially, but not making the impact you want to in the world?

WHERE DO YOU WANT TO GO?

If you ask the average person what they want from their life, and where they want to go, they will tell you what they don't want. We are wired this way. We focus on obstacles and keep running into them. In today's fast-paced, 'always on' world, we are all speeding along, trying to keep up with the demands of our lives. However, most people are flying blind; there's no GPS to help us navigate to our destination so we keep taking detours and run into potholes. We spend so much time avoiding things we're afraid of that we never get to our end destination.

What does your ideal end destination look like? Dream big. Or if this is really hard, let's break this down into manageable 'chunks'. What does your preferred life look like one year from now?

- What are you doing?

- Did you get yourself out of a toxic situation?

- Are you in control?

- Did you get your body in shape?

- Are you making more money?

- Do people gasp when you walk into a room because you radiate confidence and look amazing?

Now is the time to find clarity on where you want to go. You need to know this with complete certainty, and also why you want it. If you are currently employed – as a permanent or contracted worker – I also want you to ask yourself: are my values aligned to the organisation I work for? Can I be myself at work every day?

Many of us make the mistake of choosing goals based on what we should be doing or what society has programmed us to want and desire: 'I should get that university degree, the nine-to-five job, the perfect husband or wife, a house, cars, kids. To be successful, I must become like my toxic boss.'

In his book, *The Code of the Extraordinary Mind*, Vishen Lakhiani talks about means goals versus end goals.[16] Most people make the mistake of setting what Lakhiani calls means goals, which are things you do in order to get the experience you want to have, but which are a means to an end. An end goal is what you actually desire. In addition to identifying the experiences you want, you should be asking the following questions:

- What will help me grow and become the person I want to be?

- How can I contribute to others and the world?

- What legacy do I want to leave?

It is important to stay true to yourself, but how exactly do you stay authentic in a corporate world full of bullies? When you have a strong sense of right and wrong and when your values clash with those of the organisation and the people you work for? Here is Julie's story.

---

16   Lakhiani, V (2016) *The Code of the Extraordinary Mind: 10 unconventional laws to redefine your life and succeed on your own terms.* New York: Rodale.

JULIE'S STORY

'My mom raised me to be a strong and independent woman. She also encouraged me to always strive to do better, but despite a string of achievements, I've come to believe that it's never quite enough.

'My first bully was a woman. By treating me like a child, she thought she could control me. She used to throw things at me, refused to provide clear instructions, and slowly began to break me. After six months, my health was suffering – I stopped eating, lost a ton of weight, and each morning dreaded going into the small office I shared with her. One day, during another belittling argument, I had a moment of clarity when I stopped talking, walked out of the office and never returned. Best decision ever.

'Young and ambitious, I moved to the city. I was still studying, working crazy hours and earning very little at the time. I didn't realise that working for a living would become the norm well into my thirties. My then boss became the reason why I left a company I loved working for. I struggled to deal with his constant flirting and resigned when he told me to "do whatever it takes to get the job" after I told him that a prospective client was sexually harassing me. I was devastated.

'In my mid-thirties I settled down with my husband, and we were blessed with a baby girl. I had to return to work when she was two months old, because I'd been given a fantastic opportunity (or so I thought) by our Chief Information Officer (CIO). Thrown in at the deep end, I soon realised that the CIO had two sides to him. One was the friendly, heart-warming man I saw during presentations and social interactions, and who loved his wife and children. The other was a tyrant who was romantically involved with a team member, and who would go to great lengths to destroy anyone who got in his way, as I was soon to experience.

'When I raised my concerns over this team member's capabilities, the CIO launched a smear campaign against me, even labelling me a racist, in order to make an HR case to dismiss me. One day, after I'd sent him an email with further concerns and recommendations for improvement, he called me into his office and asked me who I thought I was to go against him and this woman. I wanted to give him a piece of my mind, but I was so shocked by his threats that I had to fight back tears. The leader who I once adored became the bully I despised. I resigned with no job to go to.

'Feeling inspired after a job interview with my future line manager – a dynamic woman around my own age – I started my current job. The first few months were amazing, until I realised that she cared only for her own career. While I did her dirty work, she took the credit. One day she pulled critical resources from my team, even though she could clearly see I was struggling and working sixteen-hour days already. She refused to discuss the matter further.

'Although I am now in charge of a multimillion-dollar finance compliance pro- gramme, it still doesn't feel quite... enough. I still deal with people (mostly men) daily who won't look at me during meetings, let alone listen to what I have to say. I have found myself working for an organisation where the culture is making it impossible for me to deliver.

'Six months ago, I began to make some changes after being ill for almost two years and feeling like I was not going to survive much longer. My daughter was growing up without a mother and my marriage was nearly over. I began seeing a psychologist and did a six-week detox with a homoeopath. Although my health has improved, I am still spending excessive hours at work, to the detriment of my family and limiting my exercise time.

'I realised that running away to another employer will not fix the issue: I want to start doing what I love. I want to feel like I am adding value again and use my experience to help managers become inspiring leaders. Over the years I have worked with many such leaders – tough yet fair and compassionate men and women. Imagine how companies can soar if leaders can think strategically and care for their people? That's why I am transitioning to a leadership coaching career, while scaling down my hours at my current employer. I am planning to work from home more often to see more of my family, and in doing so, start building the career – the life – I love. I've started to dream again about a bright future for my family. I feel so much lighter.'

Julie's story highlights how different beliefs and value systems (both of individuals and the organisations they work for) can lead to all sorts of conflicts. Knowing Julie, her strong sense of right and wrong and her fearlessness, it's perhaps not surprising that she's had quite a few run-ins with 'corporate law'. For the first time Julie is being honest with herself and beginning to visualise what her life could look like, as well as taking steps towards it. I am excited for her.

This could be you as well.

WHY DO YOU WANT IT?

Nothing happens without an emotion, or passion for something or someone. It's bigger than you. Is it your partner? Your children? Your team? Your impact on the world?

We often struggle to explain why we do what we do. What is your purpose?

- Why do you get out of bed in the morning?
- Why does your company exist?
- Why should anyone care?

Inspiring leaders and organisations, regardless of their size and industry, all start with, 'Why?'

I discovered my purpose, my why, at the age of twenty-one: to help people grow, be successful and be happy. Everyone deserves to be successful and happy – in all areas of life.

I vividly remember, on my first day as a trainee accountant with a Big Four accounting firm in Cape Town, an instant and deep desire to be the person at the front of the room, delivering the training. I also noticed the instructor's fabulous red patent leather shoes. I instinctively knew that I wanted to be in her shoes, literally and figuratively. I vividly imagined it and felt it emotionally. Usually the thought of presenting in front of people scared me. It seemed impossible at the time. I regard that day as one of those moments in my life where I was guided by grace – some attribute these moments to the Universe, others to God.

I can't remember making the decision to pursue this dream, but I became obsessed. I knew that this was what I wanted. I was on a mission because I had found a big enough why.

Over the next three years, I focused on getting as much training experience as possible. As I reached the end of my Articles, six years of blood, sweat and tears were about to pay off; I was about to qualify as a chartered accountant. The training manager position became vacant and I applied for it. Although I was up against some serious competition, I got the job. I was told afterwards that the decision was unanimous; even though my presentation was a little 'rough around the edges' (I was incredibly nervous) they saw my passion and determination. I wanted it so much and couldn't believe my luck – I was being paid to do something I absolutely loved. To this day, my most rewarding experiences have been in a classroom – teaching my students virtually or face-to-face.

The partner I worked for at the time (who I am lucky to call a dear friend today) took me under her wing. She trusted me to 'figure things out'. I knew that if I made a mistake she'd have my back. She's an incredible, visible role model. She also enrolled me on a six-month intensive voice and presentation training course (my English was shockingly bad) which changed my life. Then a fantastic opportunity came along. I was chosen to support the development of the firm's global training curriculum and shortly afterwards found myself on a plane to London for a week-long training course at which they taught us best practice training design and delivery. After working virtually with the global team for almost a year, I applied for a two-year secondment and moved to London a few months later to work as a people and change consultant.

Fast-forward almost two decades and I am still passionately pursuing my why – to help people grow, be successful and be happy. It feels like this is only the beginning. I'll never stop learning. I have big dreams for my future, which both scare and excite me.

HOW ARE YOU GOING TO GET THERE?

Just start. Have a go. Trust in your ability to figure things out. Momentum comes from a big enough why and the belief that you can and will do it. As the motivational coach Tony Robbins says, 80% of success in anything is in the psychology, and only 20% is in the mechanics.[17]

STEP 2: GAIN MOMENTUM

After I left my corporate job, I realised that it wasn't the freedom and extra money that turned my life around. Instead it was my newfound confidence, focus and energy that gave me the power to achieve everything I ever imagined. I had to let go of the past. Before I left my toxic boss, I was focusing on excuses, my string of bad luck and my adverse circumstances. All it took was a small shift in my thinking, my beliefs and my behaviour, and everything started to change for the better. Once again, I had to tame my inner bully as well.

What stories or excuses have you been telling yourself that have prevented you from achieving your best life and are keeping you stuck in your current comfort zone? Are you using a story about your past failures, telling yourself you're not good enough or smart enough, that you lack the knowledge, the time or the skills

---

17   Robbins, T (no date) 'The Psychology of a Winner: Change your psychology. Achieve unstoppable success', www.tonyrobbins.com/stories/coaching/the-psychology-of-a-winner

to achieve your goals? Or are you using the excuse that you are too young or too old or lack motivation?

Decide to end the old stories and excuses. Choose right now, today, to create a new story, telling yourself that you can succeed. You are smart enough to solve the problems that come your way. You can get the knowledge and skills you need to achieve your goals. Trust in your ability to figure things out.

Act today.

IN SUMMARY

If you know where you are, you have your starting point. Even if it is a little depressing, that's OK. Remember, all change starts with being honest. Next, figure out where you want to go. The options will narrow, and you can point your ship in the direction you really want to be going. If this means turning towards the storm, then remember that your best life is on the other side of your greatest obstacle. Focus on what you want, not what you don't want, and then figure out why you want it. Remember, you need a purpose, a cause bigger than yourself. If you don't have this clarity you cannot grow.

YOUR PURPOSE PROMPTS

- Find your 'thing'
- Be clear about your 'why'
- You are your superpower
- Trust your ability to figure it out
- Take massive action – today

FIVE

MAKE YOUR BEST LIFE A REALITY

'The credit belongs to the man who is actually in the arena, whose face is marred by the dust and sweat and blood; who strives valiantly… who, at the best, knows, in the end, the triumph of high achievement, and who, at the worst, if he fails, at least fails while daring greatly.'

THEODORE ROOSEVELT

In the previous chapter we looked at the importance of having a clear vision for your life. In this chapter I will explore what it is going to take to achieve your goals and move towards your best life. I want you to fully understand where I am coming from so that you are in the right frame of mind when setting goals and pursuing your best life. Like a springboard, the right mindset builds momentum and gives you choice, which in turn can give you freedom. If you're looking for a quick fix, then I am sorry to tell you there are not (m)any in this book. I am very much playing the longer game and recognising that success doesn't happen overnight. Be under no illusion; it will take determination, perseverance and consistency. Oh, and kindness of course.

YOUR BEST LIFE MODEL (CONTINUED)

Back to my model for living your best life.

Our focus in this chapter is on the 'how'. We'll concentrate on how to set and achieve your goals; we'll also cover the remaining three steps in the five-step process as follows:

- Create a game plan (Step 3)
- Get creative (Step 4)
- Develop capabilities (Step 5)

YOUR BEST LIFE: STEPS 3, 4 AND 5

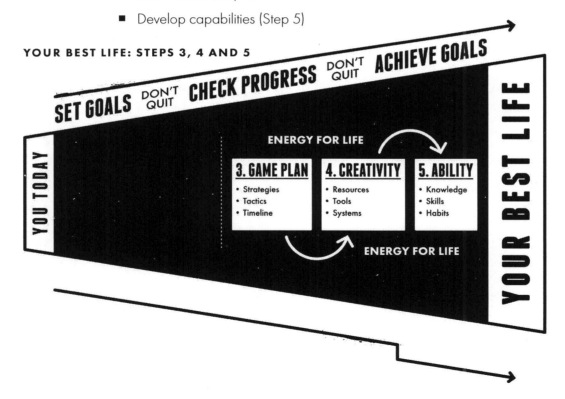

SET GOALS

I want you to look back one day and say, 'Oh my goodness, what a journey!' To do that you have to set goals.

Ask yourself: what gets me out of bed in the morning? What gets me fired up? If what you want to achieve touches on that, even if you're a little scared or uncertain, you'll overcome struggles and setbacks in order to achieve what you want.

When setting goals, you have two options. You can:

1. Set goals that stretch you a little bit

    -   Pros: It's a lot easier, you won't be overwhelmed and it's a great starting point.

    -   Cons: May take longer, you may not attract the big thinkers and needed resources, you won't grow as fast.

2. Set goals that stretch you a lot

    -   Pros: You will attract and resonate with the people and resources required. You will achieve far beyond your perceived potential. You will fail faster and learn at a rapid rate.

    -   Cons: The likelihood is that you will be extremely stressed, overwhelmed and much more confused. The complexity of this approach requires absolute and relentless mental and emotional control. The risks of failure are much greater.

When I decided to write this book, I had no idea how I was going to do it and I definitely experienced a lot of stress and the sense of being overwhelmed.

However, I was determined to do it. I had a big enough why: to help people tame the bully – the one on the inside and the one on the outside.

Regardless of your goal – whether it is building a business, getting healthier, improving a relationship or writing a book – you can achieve anything, provided you believe you can (as discussed in Chapter Four) and provided you are committed.

ARE YOU INTERESTED OR ARE YOU COMMITTED?

If you're interested, you'll do what is convenient and easy. You are going to come up with stories and excuses for why you don't have time, why it's too hard, why it's too complicated. Stories and excuses are reasons not to do things.

However, if you are committed, you'll do whatever it takes. You'll understand your strengths and weaknesses; you'll upgrade your knowledge, skills and beliefs. You'll change your habits and learn self-discipline. You'll become obsessed. Immerse yourself. Do whatever it takes.

If you are serious and committed, over time, you can achieve any goal you want. If you are prepared to go through the discomfort of change for long enough to create a new pattern and a new paradigm, then you can achieve each and every one of your goals.

STEP 3: CREATE A GAME PLAN

You need a game plan, a so-called 'plan of attack' – a series of strategies and tactics you can deploy in order to reach your goal. You also need a timeline in which to achieve this.

Does SMART ring a bell? It's a common way to set goals: they should be Specific, Measurable, Achievable, Relevant and Time-bound. You should consider whether your goals fit these descriptors and use them as ways to refine your aims.

At the outset of writing my book, I knew that in order to finish it I was going to have to become extremely productive; juggling a family, a business, my own wellness and writing a book is no small feat. I discovered a simple model by Brendon Burchard whereby he teaches us to break each goal into five major moves towards achievement. Then you have to break each move into activities, steps and deadlines. These were my five major moves that were going to get my book published:

1. Finish writing a good book. Until that's done, nothing else matters.

2. Get an agent or self-publish.

3. Start blogging and posting to social media.

4. Create a book promotion web page and offer some appealing bonus material.

5. Get five to ten people to promote the book.

Finding these five moves saved me lots of time (thank you Brendon!). Don't try to reinvent the wheel – whatever your goal, someone's done it before. Learn from them and trust the process.

Start by answering a question:

- What does your best life look like?

- Now set a goal or goals that will move you towards this life.

- Develop a game plan:
  - Chart your five major moves.
  - Identify the activities, steps and deadlines for each.

STEP 4: GET CREATIVE

Your most powerful resource is your own creativity – generating new ideas, visualising the outcome and making things happen by getting the necessary tools and systems in place.

But what if you are not creative? Where does this leave you?

I recently had a conversation with my cousin Mia, telling me exactly that: 'I am not creative.' You see, Mia comes from a family of creatives. Andre, her dad, is an artist – I have four of his paintings in my house. Wanda, her mom, is an entrepreneur and co-founder of KAMERS/Makers, South Africa's original artisan pop-up market.[18] Andre-Leo, Mia's brother, is a musician. Mia decided that she wanted to become a chartered accountant and is now studying BAcc[19] at the University of Stellenbosch, exactly the same thing I did (over twenty years ago now).

Mia is one of the most creative people I know. She's an incredible dancer and blogger, and fashion has always been her thing. Music has always been my thing. In my final year of school, I got a distinction in my Grade 8 piano exam,

---

18 https://kamersvol.com
19 www.sun.ac.za/english/faculty/economy/accounting/programmes/academic-programmes/bacc-bacchons-chartered-accountant-(ca)

and I probably would have ended up being a piano teacher if I didn't change my mind literally weeks before I went to university.

You see, creativity is so much more than just art and music. Creativity is at the heart of everything on our planet, including wealth, success and abundance. Think of the word creativity; the root is 'create'. Just as you can take a pen, a paintbrush, or many other tools and create a work of art, so can you use any number of tools to create new and amazing wealth. The process is essentially the same. The more creative you are, the easier it is to create your best life.

This is a massive part of my modus operandi. To me, creativity is everything. It is something that every single individual on this planet is born with, with zero exceptions. Every thought that enters your head is a creation. Every word you utter is created by you. Every word you write or type is an act of creativity. When you feel emotions, they are your creations. Every man-made thing on this planet was once an idea, a thought in someone's mind, and it eventually became a creation, a work of creativity.

Take a moment to visualise all of the good things that will happen to you as you achieve your best life. As you experience these feelings, persistence will build within you. Whenever I do this exercise I think about my own kids – especially my youngest – who rarely have the personal ability to achieve the things they desire on their own. However, when they make up their minds that they want something, they will continue to use whatever limited resources they have and push forward at every opportunity. Why do adults, who have many more resources than children, rarely have extreme persistence? Try to remember a time that you desired something so intensely that you would have done anything to get it, and the result was that you did – somehow. It's time to reignite your inner child and get creative.

STEP 5: DEVELOP CAPABILITIES

If you wait until you have the skills to pursue any goal, it's highly unlikely that you'll ever achieve it. You have to trust in your ability to figure things out. That's why I put ability last in the order of essential steps.

Get comfortable feeling uncomfortable. Just start – have a go – and ask yourself: what do I need to learn? What skills and habits do I need to develop?

I don't know about you, but in terms of living my best life, I aspire to play at the pro level. I know that it will take a lot more blood, sweat and tears in the coming years. There will be many ups and downs, but progress, nonetheless. It doesn't matter how long it takes. What matters is that you don't quit.

Also, you should not just aspire to get it right; aim to get so good that you can no longer get it wrong. As I am writing this Roger Federer and Novak Djokovic are playing in the Wimbledon 2019 final. The press is calling it 'a clash of giants' and they're now at the third set tie break. Federer is 5–1 down. As a massive Federer fan my stress levels are through the roof and I am unable to watch right now. This is as good as it gets.

My point? That these guys are so brilliant, they hardly get it wrong anymore – to be able to play at the pro level for so long is just mind-blowing. They have incredible mental and physical strength. To me, they are the epitome of high performance.

Ask yourself these questions:

- What are your strengths?
- What are your weaknesses (or perceived weaknesses)?
- What is it you really need?

You may be saying, 'I don't know what my weaknesses are, I don't know what my strengths are, I don't know what I need.'

Great. What has to happen in order for you to know? Who do you need to ask? Who can help you? What can you read? What YouTube videos can you watch? What training can you do? You have to be resourceful, regardless of your resources.

Commit today.

CHECK PROGRESS

What I've learned over the years is that taking small daily steps towards achieving your goals consistently, will deliver mind-blowing results before you know it. That's why I love the saying, 'How do you eat an elephant? One bite at a time.' As long as you approach it with the right mindset, regularly check progress, and don't quit, you will get there. Even if you can't see or feel it, trust that you are making progress. Just make it happen, don't negotiate with yourself, get up and do it – whatever it is – every day. If you need to, get an accountability partner or coach.

I first discovered the value of a coach when I decided to get my physical and mental health back on track after my bullying experience left me at rock bottom. It was the best decision I've ever made – not only did I get results; I've also been able to sustain them. When I decided to write this book, I planned to do it on my own, but soon realised that I needed someone to hold me accountable and provide expert advice to get me through the book writing process.

My game plan for publishing this book is currently on its fourth iteration. Although my five moves haven't changed, I'm constantly reassessing, refocusing and adjusting my activities and timelines. I've come to learn during this process that writing is a creative, messy process. Some of the delays I am experiencing are down to life getting in the way, good old writer's block, the need for additional research, physical exhaustion, and the nonsense I make myself believe. Thank goodness for my book coach. I submitted my final book draft to the publisher six months after I decided to work with a coach. I know this would not have been possible had I tried to do it on my own.

Which brings me to the most important attribute of all: that you don't quit on yourself.

DON'T QUIT

How resilient are you? How big is your quit muscle? Do you quit whenever things get hard? When you get confused, overwhelmed or you just don't feel like it?

If you want to master goal achievement, you'll need a miniscule quit muscle. The only things you should stop doing are the things that don't work; you must not quit on yourself.

You've set goals. You've committed. You've gone off track. It's normal. Just don't quit. If necessary, reset, readjust, restart, refocus your goal(s) – as many times as you need to.

Here is a quick reality check for you. The level of difficulty you face typically represents the level of success you crave. If you are satisfied with an average life, a decent job, an OK relationship and your body looking all right, then life is going to be a lot easier than for someone who wants to maximise their fullest potential – run their own business or rise through the ranks in their organisation, have an amazing relationship, a fantastic body, be an incredible parent, thrive and find happiness – those take more problems. If you say you don't want problems, you're really saying that you don't want success. Problems are the building blocks of success. To reach your full potential, you have to figure things out.

Failure is a feedback loop, showing you which thoughts, emotions or behaviours aren't working. It is not a reflection on you as a person; it just means that you didn't do the right things in the right order at the right time. Trust me, you have more power than you think you do.

What will it take to achieve your goals?

ACHIEVE YOUR GOALS

If you are currently in a bullying situation or stuck – for whatever reason – there is a good chance that you are holding yourself back. It's likely to be rooted in one or more of three things:

1. Self-esteem or self-image issues – eg I am not smart or good enough; I don't know how; I don't deserve it; I am not worthy; I am too old or too young.

2. Fears – eg fear of taking action, fear of being judged or ridiculed, fear of change, fear of failure, fear of success, of rejection, of disappointment, or of what others might think.

3. Self-limiting beliefs, stories and excuses – eg I don't have the skills, resources or time; I am not creative; I don't know how to start a business; I don't have enough money; I am not lucky like other people; it's too late for me to find happiness and success; I should be further along; I am not destined to be rich; it's selfish to put my needs before others.

Ask yourself the following:

- Am I procrastinating a lot?

- Am I constantly talking negatively to myself?

- Am I constantly feeling confused, overwhelmed, and that it is all too much?

These are signs of neural dissonance. It means that you have a subconscious block that will override a conscious goal, vision or even your 'why'. Back off a little bit, so that there is less pressure on you. Recalibrate and take some action. If you activate the fear circuit in your brain you need to know how to respond effectively.

It is normal to have fears. What is not normal is for you to become a victim of your fear and for it to hold you back. Fears are subconscious emotions that trigger a neuro-electrical release. When we are feeling uncertain, we feel this anxiety. We want to stop and retreat to safety. I want you to be more in control of what is happening in your head and your heart so that you are in the driver's seat.

IN SUMMARY

We have now covered the steps that I believe are essential for making your best life a reality. To summarise: find (or reignite) your purpose, gain momentum, set goals, create a game plan, get creative, develop your capabilities, check your progress and don't quit until you achieve your goals. Achieving your goals will require relentless pursuit. You may change your strategies, tactics and timing, but don't quit until you achieve your goals. Depending on how big your goal is, you may find that the process goes on for the rest of your life. In order to achieve your goals and best life, you will have to:

- Win the inner game (your psychology – Chapter Six)
- Win the outer game (your physiology – Chapter Seven)

Know this: within you is everything you need to achieve all of your goals and dreams.

YOUR BEST LIFE PROMPTS

- **Dream big**
- **Be scared**
- **Have a go anyway**
- **Fail, but don't quit**
- **Figure out a new way**

SIX

WIN THE INNER GAME

**'Our only limitations
are those we set up in
our own minds.'**

NAPOLEON HILL

You are now familiar with my model for living your best life. We briefly
touched on the importance of developing empowering beliefs and habits
to overcome self-doubt, fear, old stories and excuses.

In this chapter we will look at the psychology of the brain – your inner game –
and specifically how the brain works. You have to control your brain; otherwise
it will control you.

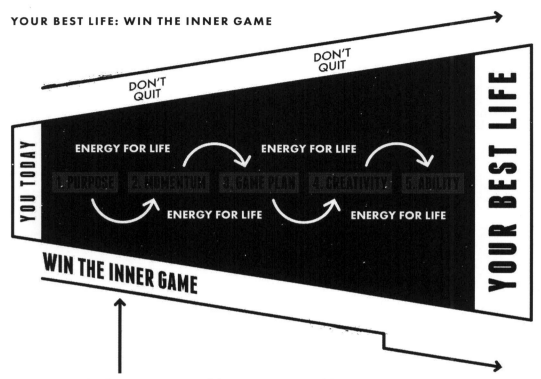

The brain is so powerful. It is programmed for safety first; it wants us to quit, to maintain the status quo and not to take risks. If we move out of our comfort zone it talks to us negatively, uses self-deprecating language, and creates emotions and behaviours that don't serve us.

Take fear, for example. Fear comes from the reptilian brain, the emotional response centre of the brain (subconscious) that notices any change in our surroundings or circumstances. If it senses any real or potential danger, the subconscious emotion causes a conscious feeling. When we say feel anxious, our motivation decreases. We stop and go back to safety. That's why 'old habits die hard'.

This makes it essential to control and 'rewire' our brains. In the same way that we must eat healthily and exercise regularly to keep our bodies fit and strong, we also have to 'innercise'[20] our minds to become psychologically strong and flexible. In this way we can build mental resilience, or 'mind over matter'.

Winning the inner game means understanding the power that is already within you. We have amazing, unbridled potential inside us. We just have to learn how to use our brains better, prime them properly and take small steps every day. If you're not used to lifting heavy weights, start lighter. If you're not used to running, start by walking. Just start.

HOW THE BRAIN WORKS

My months of research made me realise just how little we know about how the brain works.

At birth we are given an amazing natural computer, but few of us have been taught how to use it. Like a real computer, we're expected to just figure it out. Some of us break or damage our computers along the way.

A friend I spoke to recently is having a tough time with her teenage daughter. She said: 'Marilise, I just feel like a failure.' I took her through my simple 'Think – Feel – Say – Act' process.

---

20 Assaraf, J (2018) *Innercise: The new science to unlock your brain's hidden power.* Cardiff, CA: Waterside.

THINK – FEEL – SAY – ACT

·INNER GAME·

1. THINK   2. FEEL

4. ACT   3. SAY

·OUTER GAME·

In order to feel like a failure, she had to first think 'I am a failure'. I asked her to give me a more empowering thought – or positive affirmation – to which she responded: 'I am a good mother; I do my best every day.' Then she smiled and her body language immediately changed – she stood a little taller.

Every one of us is a human system; we have a mind, body, spirit and soul. Everything is interconnected. How we think, and then feel, will ultimately guide how we behave. For example:

- We feel hungry – we eat
- We feel tired – we don't exercise
- We feel anxious – our breathing gets shallow
- We feel like a bad parent – we lash out

The important thing to realise is that your feelings are not in charge. We only ever feel what we are thinking. Thinking will only ever do one of two things: it will either work for you, or against you. The metaphor I use is the story of Simba and Scar from *The Lion King*, my favourite movie and play. I love the African savanna, the rhythmic beats, the glorious animals and bold colours. It is the story of good (Simba) and evil (Scar), and a destructive jealousy. The beauty of the natural world is restored when the hero returns to take back his kingdom. Perhaps it's no coincidence that the remake of *The Lion King* has recently launched in cinemas. Gosh, has it really been twenty-five years?

When the conversations I have with myself are calm, courageous and caring, Simba is in the driving seat, but when self-hatred, fears, limiting beliefs, excuses and old stories cripple me, Scar takes over.

Which brings me to the conscious and subconscious mind. This is where it gets really intriguing, because the subconscious mind is responsible for 95–99% of our cognitive activity and therefore controls almost all of our decisions, actions, emotions and behaviours.[21] The subconscious mind is made up of every piece

---

21   Szegedy-Maszak, M (2005) 'Mysteries of the Mind: Your unconscious is making your everyday decisions', http://webhome.auburn.edu/~mitrege/ENGL2210/USNWR-mind.html; Lipton, B (2014) 'What Do You Want to Learn About the Subconscious Mind?' www.brucelipton.com/blog/what-do-you-want-learn-about-the-subconscious-mind

of information you've ever received since the day you were born. We absorb around two million pieces of information per second. We don't know what is happening in our subconscious brain.

Imagine a filing cabinet with the top drawer as your conscious thoughts. As you go down through the lower drawers you are reaching further into your subconscious.

HOW MY THOUGHTS NEARLY DESTROYED ME

MY EATING DISORDER – HOW IT ALL STARTED

Shortly after I exposed the man who sexually abused me and my sister, I became aware of my body, and of feeling ashamed. As in every small town, the story spread like wildfire. Everyone knew. Every time a boy looked at me, I felt self-conscious; I felt like damaged goods and as though I was slowly dying on the inside. On the outside I was my parents' responsible eldest daughter – academic, creative, sporty and popular. I had to be strong for my family, who were falling apart after the news. I insisted that I didn't need help and managed to convince my parents that I was fine. In South Africa in the 1980s, sexual abuse was swept under the carpet; no one spoke openly about it (much like workplace bullying today). I grew up in a 'just get a grip' era – mental health wasn't something we knew or spoke about.

MY UNHEALTHY RELATIONSHIP WITH FOOD AND EXERCISE BEGINS

At thirteen I was taller and bigger than most of the girls in my class, and very muscular and sporty. I was self-conscious about my round face and chubby cheeks. One day a boy commented on my big bum and I made it official in my head:

I am fat. It started with a thought, then a feeling, and then I started believing it. My subsequent actions almost killed me.

I started exercising obsessively, sometimes three times a day. On some days I survived on just water and an apple. One Saturday, after I couldn't finish a netball match, my worried parents took me to the doctor. He showed me that my blood pressure and blood sugar levels were too low compared with a healthy person's. This frightened me and I agreed to start eating. However, anyone who has suffered from an eating disorder, or indeed any addiction, will know that it doesn't work like that. Treating the symptom by forcing myself to eat only made matters worse. I was still fat, or so I believed, and exercising compulsively. Unfortunately, I was also now eating compulsively. I eventually developed full-blown bulimia.

Things got worse when I went to university, and by the end of my third year I was out of control and purging multiple times a day. I still don't know how I managed to complete my degree. I couldn't stay in a house with other people – I would eat all of their food, which filled me with shame – so I moved in with my grandmother, Ouma Marie. She was the most amazing woman and my second mother; my parents had been students when I was born so my grandparents looked after me during the day.

Around the time I moved in with Ouma Marie, she was diagnosed with terminal breast and skin cancer. One evening, I caught her scratching her itchy back with a ruler, so I offered to help her. Frustrated and heartbroken, I couldn't understand why she always said she was fine, while suffering behind closed doors. I understand now that a parent will do anything to protect a child from pain and suffering. That evening, with deep worry in her eyes, she asked me to promise her that I would be OK. I promised.

This, combined with failing my final tax exam, ultimately led to my decision to go to rehab. By that point, I'd seen psychologist after psychologist and lost count of the number of Prozac prescriptions I'd had. I realised that nobody else could save me. I realised that I had to take control before the Scar part of my character killed me. I had to do it for Ouma Marie, just like I did it for my sister all those years ago. I had a why that was bigger than myself.

THE ROAD TO RECOVERY BEGINS

Saying goodbye at the entrance to the rehab clinic broke my mom's heart. That day, she realised for the first time just how ill – mentally and physically – her eldest daughter was, even though I could still do nothing wrong in her eyes. She recently told me that she felt responsible. Was it the sexual abuse? Was it my personality type? Was it because she idolised me? Was it because of her own poor self-image and disordered eating? Did she set an unhealthy example?

This is where I'd like to interrupt the story for a moment to say: 'Mom, you are exactly the reason why I am where I am today. You taught me to be strong and independent, and to stand in my power. As a woman in a man's world you showed me that it is possible to have a successful career and also be an amazing mother and wife. You and Ouma Marie paid it forward for us girls. We can't be what we can't see, so thank you.'

The toughest thing about rehab was not being able to exercise; we were only allowed a short walk every other day. I was used to two to three hours of exercise every day. I had to eat everything on my plate and was not allowed to go to the bathroom afterwards. Other than that, I felt quite 'normal' compared to the other patients; my problems were small compared to most of them. I was surrounded by very ill people. This broke my heart. It was the wake-up call I so desperately needed.

GETTING A GRIP ON MY ANXIETY

By beginning to understand my thoughts, I also began to understand my anxiety for the first time. I constantly worried about things – even if I had no control over them – and I was always expecting the worst. I realised that my worries and negative thoughts weren't real, although they felt it. Remember: think – feel – say – act.

This was when I met Simba and Scar – the two voices in my head – for the first time. When I was performing at my best Simba was in control; but by now, Scar was pretty much in the driving seat every day, comprising all the limiting beliefs, fears, excuses and stories I told myself. I was punishing myself – I felt ashamed and guilty of the deceit and hurt I had inflicted along the way.

Rehab saved me from self-destruction. It interrupted the patterns of behaviour I had hardwired into my brain over a period of almost ten years. It taught me how to interrupt these patterns and replace them with empowering beliefs and habits. Our daily meditation sessions taught me the power of private reflection, silence, solitude and stillness.

Shortly after rehab I was given another chance at sitting my tax exam. My amazing dad, who had got me out of trouble numerous times before, explained my situation to the lecturer. I passed and got my degree. I was about to start my corporate career, with a Big Four accounting firm.

It took me another few years to fully recover; I had many relapses. The turning point for me came when I met my husband, which I will tell you more about in the next chapter. To be brutally honest, I don't think you ever fully recover from such an illness. In addition to managing my mindset, I also have to carefully manage my nutrition and exercise, which is what Chapter Seven is all about. Fortunately,

Scar is a lot quieter these days; sometimes he doesn't appear at all. I know he will never completely go away, but that's OK.

THE NEUROSCIENCE BEHIND OUR ACTIONS

It was an eye opener to realise that it's my subconscious brain that drives me. When I hit the snooze button or talk myself out of doing something like writing this book (a frequent occurrence), my conscious and subconscious brain are not working together in harmony. I was intrigued to discover this and wanted to understand the neuroscience behind my actions better.

I learned that the reason for everything we do is based in neuroscience. The very act of learning more about neuroscience can help us to overcome the subconscious blockers – self-esteem issues, fears and limiting beliefs – that may hold us back. This is important because a subconscious block will override a conscious desire, goal, vision or even a 'why'.

Let's look at neuroscience in the context of setting goals and achieving goals. What is the difference between the two?

To set goals, we use conscious brain activities such as deductive reasoning, imagination, perception, intuition and desire. This takes place in the top part of the brain, the neocortex – the logical, rational, thinking part of the brain.

To achieve goals, we need to create alignment between our conscious and subconscious brain activities, which include empowering beliefs and habits, a 'no matter what' mindset, self-discipline, emotional management, adaptability and persistence.

If you set goals, you activate the left prefrontal cortex (for me this is Simba), but right after that the fear response centre (for me it's Scar) lights up and you start to feel disempowered. You may experience disempowering thoughts or emotions, fear, self-doubt, overwhelm, confusion and stress. This is how the conversation may play out:

> SIMBA: I am going to [stretch goal]. I am excited, motivated, fired up, I know can do it. This is why I have to [vision], because [why].

> SCAR: What have you done? What if you fail? What if you embarrass yourself? What if...

See the struggle? This chaos in the brain is called neural dissonance – the uncertainty gap between where you are and where you want to be.

The emotional part of the brain (the fear response centre) is the brake or the accelerator. When you have too much change going on, it creates neural dissonance; you have one foot on the accelerator (logical brain) and one foot on the brake (emotional brain), so you're going to be spinning your wheels.

To achieve any goal, we need to get all parts of the brain working coherently. Notice the neural dissonance and manage it accordingly. Two of the easiest emotions to recognise are overwhelm and confusion.

GET ORGANISED WHEN YOU FEEL OVERWHELMED

When everything feels 'too much' I want you to stop and recalibrate; create an organised, sequential plan of what has to happen first, second, third and so on. When you are feeling overwhelmed, you feel like everything is happening at the same time, and you can't keep track of it in your head. It's like having too many tabs open on your computer – you need to close some. Transfer the chaos out of your head onto a piece of paper (or a computer) first, then create a plan of what you are going to do in the next twenty-four hours; ideally three action points. This will help to reduce or eliminate the sensation of being overwhelmed.

GET COMFORTABLE FEELING CONFUSED

Confusion just means concepts getting fused. The new concepts that are being fused together require energy, and when you're experiencing energy depletion, many people feel uncomfortable. Guess what? You're actually growing. Get comfortable feeling uncomfortable.

When we are learning new knowledge, skills and habits, we are forming new connections in the brain. Sometimes our brains get overwhelmed and want to disconnect. Why? We have a finite number of attention units and any time we get outside of our attention unit zone, we have to use willpower, a limited resource, to stay focused; this is where those persistence muscles are necessary.

Remember, our brains are wired for safety first and want to protect us from the unpleasant emotions and disempowering thoughts that are activated when we change our behaviour to move towards our goals. Keep going for as long as it takes.

At some point your subconscious brain will realise: 'She keeps doing it – it must be important to her.' It will stop putting on the brakes. Our brains are stubborn but they eventually see the light and follow the path of least resistance. A lot of our actions start as conscious choices, but with practice you can go from conscious competence to unconscious competence, effectively creating alignment between your conscious and subconscious minds. This is when you hit your flow state.

START BY GIVING YOURSELF PERMISSION

A highly accomplished cybersecurity executive recently told me this: 'I now understand that the deep fear that drives all of my protective mechanisms is standing in the way of me being my true self. The fear is that people will find out that I am worthless.'

She was not the first highly accomplished leader to tell me this; I've been hearing it a lot. It's called imposter syndrome. This is how self-doubt, fears and limiting beliefs often manifest themselves, particularly in the corporate world. I also suffer from it. Here is just one example of how it appeared recently.

Early on, when planning my book with my coach, I expressed that I often wonder: why me? What makes me credible enough to be writing about high performance? I listed the names of some of the world leading experts on this topic, and I started to feel anxious. The first time I mentioned this worry, my coach let it go, but the second time there was a pause and then she asked my permission to intervene.

I agreed and she continued: 'Here I am with a woman who has just finished training with Brendon Burchard. You are now a Certified High Performance Coach. Not only that, you're an accredited Liberating Leadership Practitioner. You've also held a directorship in a company in the research field, and you are a qualified accountant. I feel secure that I have an expert in the room with me who has her own ideas about high performance. I want to move you beyond the books you've been reading and the people you feel empowered by, OK? I just want you to talk – off the top of your head – about what high performance is and what it means to you.'

LET GO OF THE IMPOSTER

Imposter syndrome is one way in which our deep-rooted limiting beliefs manifest themselves. What are your limiting beliefs? What stories have you been telling yourself? What excuses are you using?

You're dealing with the most powerful computer on the planet, in an era where you can Google the answer to literally anything in seconds. It doesn't matter what situation you currently find yourself in; you can achieve anything your heart desires if you can let go of your self-esteem issues, fears, limiting beliefs, excuses and old stories.

As we've seen in this chapter, what matters the most is what happens in your brain. It is going to dictate your emotions, thoughts, feelings and behaviours, so you have to be alert to what's happening.

- What's causing you to be motivated and move forward?
- What's causing you to put on the brake and get stuck?

Reframe your thoughts to develop empowering beliefs and habits. A limiting belief is a pattern in the brain, which will always be there. You cannot get rid of it completely, but by being aware of what's happening in your mind and body, you can stop the limiting belief from automatically creating a negative thought. You can recreate a new positive thought – an empowering belief – and if you continue for long enough, it will become the new default pattern. The negative thought doesn't go away; your brain just follows the path of least resistance by making the positive thought automatic and pushing the negative thought aside. You create a new habit.

IN SUMMARY

Your past or present circumstances do not equal your future. The person you are today cannot – must not – be defined by your past. Delete the past. This is mastering your life, but you have to understand that you are responsible. You have the ability to change.

Whatever happened in the past is exactly that – in the past – but you can use things that happened in the past as your guiding point and reference to make better decisions in the future.

Start making your inner game work for you – today.

INNER GAME PROMPTS

- Recognise the power of 'mind over matter'
- Catch negative self-talk sooner
- Reframe your thoughts – be positive and grateful
- See the possibilities
- Put your past behind you

SEVEN

WIN THE OUTER GAME

> 'Your smile is your logo. Your personality is your business card. How you leave others feeling after having an experience with you becomes your trademark.'
>
> **JAY DANZIE**

In the previous chapter, we looked at the mind part of our human system (our psychology). In this chapter, we'll look at the other three parts – body, spirit and soul (our physiology).

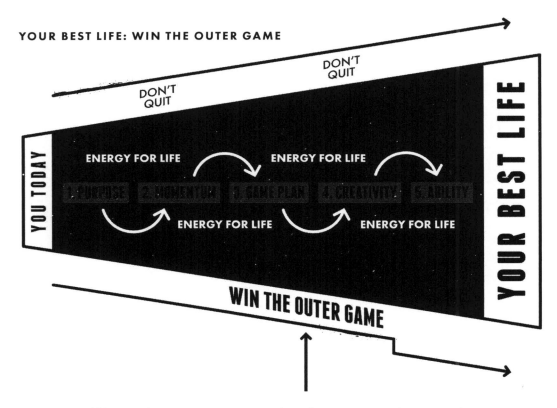

Winning the outer game – your physiology – starts with winning the inner game. A strong mind enables a strong body. For me, winning the outer game is all about:

- How I show up every day – as a mom, a wife, a leader – always as the best version of me

- Generating the energy to show up – my nutrition and exercise – my two non-negotiables

Why was getting into the best shape of my life important to me? How do I manage my human system every day, to stay in control by de-stressing and generate that energy?

For starters, I don't have much of choice. It is not possible for me to juggle an important job, write a book and run a household without being in control of how I fuel my body and de-stress (or decompress).

I have incredible support systems, especially at home; all credit to my husband, Heinie – I could not do what I do without him. We take an equal share of all parenting and household duties, although he might argue that he does a little bit more (especially when I do crazy things, like writing a book for example).

I know what happens if I don't take care of myself. It was only after I crashed and burned that I realised just how much my support systems – at home and at work – depend on me showing up mentally and physically strong, every single day. When I fell apart, my support systems almost fell apart too.

It's never too late, and I hope my story will inspire you to take action – small steps even – if you're finding yourself in an unhappy, unfulfilled place. I'll jump straight in.

MY STORY (CONTINUED)

After rehab and on the road to recovery at last, I was now working in a Big Four accounting firm and loving it. Here is a quick summary of some key life events – each filled with ups, downs and lessons learned – in the fifteen (or so) years before I met my bully.

Life event	Lesson learned
Qualifying as a chartered accountant	Education opens doors; self-education keeps them open
Finding my why	Find something you love so much that you become obsessed
Meeting Heinie, moving to London	My perspective is not the perspective
Becoming a mom	Family is everything
Climbing the corporate ladder	Don't try to fit in if you're born to stand out
'Falling' into cybersecurity	Constant and never-ending learning

I am now taking a moment to breathe and reflect on how far I've come. I can't help but smile. It's been an incredible journey (and continues to be). I wouldn't be the person I am today without these incredible life events and learning experiences along the way.

Let's pick up the story where I crossed paths with a bully whose verbal and emotional abuse reawakened Scar, the negative voice in my head, and how it almost destroyed me.

WHY DIDN'T I SEE THIS ONE COMING?

It is an unavoidable fact that I worked for a bully. I didn't necessarily understand it at the time and I share, in Chapter One, five reasons why it took me almost four years to walk away. With these five reasons, I did a lot of introspection. One thing I didn't do was to remind myself why he wanted me to work for him in the first place, which was the fact that I am an amazing people and change leader.

I quickly became his highest performing manager and built excellent relationships with my team and our clients. However, deep inside I hated every minute of every day – because of him. I am sure he saw it as 'tough love and character building'. He had a stereotypical 'control and command' leadership approach. I think he honestly believed he was doing me a favour – that it was going to make me tougher and more like him.

It did make me tougher, for a while. At first, blinded by my ambition, I would do anything to please him and 'fix things'. I am ashamed to say that I even began mirroring his behaviour for a while, until my eyes opened and I saw his true colours. I realised that he wasn't just being demanding, he was demeaning everyone. For a while I wondered whether this was my new normal, if perhaps when you got to a certain level, you just had 'take it on the chin'.

Fortunately, I had worked with enough exceptional leaders along the way to realise that his behaviour wasn't normal. It wasn't normal to feel sick every day before work or to be scared of having a conversation with your boss for fear of him shouting you down or belittling you in front of everyone. I lost count of the number of times this happened. Every time I thought it could not possibly get any worse, he pulled something else out of the hat. The straw that broke the camel's back was the day he effectively demoted me – in front of my entire team – with no prior warning.

I remember it like yesterday. I was sitting in a boardroom full of people, my team, when he dropped the bombshell. In his usual 'I know what's best for everyone' way, he announced that instead of managing the team and our portfolio, I was going to work on one project until that project delivered. He was going to step in to do my role temporarily 'to save the day'. Yes, the project was in trouble and I was OK with that. Then he announced the imminent arrival of a new person. I realised this wasn't just a temporary arrangement. It felt like being punched in the stomach.

Assuming I knew about this arrangement beforehand, people started asking questions. They talked about me as if I wasn't in the room. I didn't say a single word throughout the whole meeting; I was done fighting – mentally and physically defeated. I looked down the entire time, too ashamed to make eye contact with anyone. Scar was having a field day. Straight after this dreadful meeting, I got in touch with HR and my exit was swiftly agreed. A few months before I left, my eating disorder had been threatening to stick its head out. I sought professional help and discovered the devastating impact stress was having on my body.

I believe the only thing that saved me throughout the bullying experience was exercise. I was training for Ride London, a 100-mile cycling tour, so I had no choice but to get my backside in the saddle every weekend. Unfortunately, exercising compulsively once a week wasn't healthy either. Due to chronic stress, I developed adrenal fatigue. My adrenal glands were not producing enough cortisol; this is the hormone which helps the body respond to stress, and it also regulates a range of vital processes throughout the body, including metabolism and the immune response.

Even though I was just about able to control my food intake, wine became my new drug of choice and my anaesthetic. I was treating the symptom once again. No wonder I was getting fat, despite being fit. I was roughly 1.5 stone (9.5kgs) heavier than my normal, healthy weight. I was a ticking time-bomb.

The morning after the 100-mile ride, for the first time in almost eight years, I found myself on the scale. I am petrified of scales. I saw the number and panicked. I was also reminded of a picture of myself on Facebook from the day before –

standing in front of Buckingham Palace, above the caption: 'I did it'. Instead of feeling proud of my achievement, I felt disgusted with the way I looked.

I was unemployed, without purpose, and fat. My personal relationships were hanging by a thread. For the second time in my life, I'd reached rock bottom.

How did I get myself into such a mess?

THE ROAD TO RECOVERY BEGINS (TAKE TWO)

For the first time since moving to the UK I was not commuting to London on a busy train every day. Instead, I took the kids to school once or twice. I hated it. I felt completely lost. I was having an identity crisis – my big corporate job had become such a major part of who I was that I felt completely lost. The boys had got used to coping without their mom and I felt completely redundant. I felt utterly out of place and deeply confused. Scar was wreaking havoc. I was so unhappy that I struggled to drag myself out of bed in the mornings.

After about two weeks of staying in my pyjamas most days, one morning I forced myself to get up and out. I started going to the gym. It was hard in the beginning, but I instinctively knew that I needed to take control of my nutrition and exercise first and foremost. If rehab taught me one thing, it was to interrupt that downward spiral of self-destructive thoughts, feelings and habits. I was petrified of going back to that deep, dark place.

Remember my three steps from Chapter Four? Get honest, get clear, get help.

My three-month stint on gardening leave gave me time to regain some perspective on life. I was really honest with myself about my situation, and I started gaining clarity about the ideal life I wanted to create. By now I'd started my own business and lined up my first client. However, I was haunted by that picture of myself after my cycle ride, so I set myself a goal: to get into the best shape of my life, for life.

I decided to get help. I realised it was not something I could attempt on my own. My first step towards achieving my goal was to invest in a transformation coach – the ridiculously talented and inspirational Colette Pienaar. It was a great decision, and one that accelerated my results. I achieved my goal of getting into the best shape of my life within four months; I managed to drop from 27% to 14.5% body fat. It's because of the 'for life' part of the goal that I still work with Colette today. It's no longer about losing weight, but instead staying lean and building muscle. It's about creating energy for life, and staying mentally and physically strong and healthy.

Colette also helps me face one of my biggest fears – she encourages me to hop on the scales every two weeks for my usual weigh and measure. Being confronted with 'that number' still petrifies me, without fail, but I do it.

Remember think, then feel, then act? This brings me to three daily mindset shifts you can make:

1. Put yourself – your health – first

2. Manage your stress levels – decompress

3. Diarise 'me time' and do not cancel on yourself

Let's go through each in a bit more detail.

PUT YOURSELF – YOUR HEALTH – FIRST

Take some time to understand what your nutrition and training needs look like for your particular body type.[22]

- Ectomorph: lean and long, with difficulty building muscle

- Endomorph: big, high body fat, often pear-shaped, with high tendency to store body fat

- Mesomorph: muscular and well built, with high metabolism and responsive muscle cells

There is a reason why people say that 'you are what you eat'. It really is 80% about food and 20% about exercise. If you are one of those people who exercises to eat and drink what you want, unfortunately it doesn't work like that. Even though we all know this, as Brendon's training always reminds me, 'common sense is not always common practice'.[23]

When I started my body transformation programme, I went onto an elimination plan: no wheat, dairy, coffee, alcohol, red meat or refined sugars for thirty days. I learned about specific food groups and how they affected my body. I learned about drinking enough water, and the importance of sleep, supplementation and eating frequently. These actions gave me the kick-start that I needed. This is also where I saw a lot of my weight loss. Despite my history with eating disorders and

22   Snape, J (2017) 'Ectomorph, Endomorph and Mesomorph: How to train for your body type', *Coach Magazine*, 1 September, www.coachmag.co.uk/lifestyle/4511/ectomorph-endomorph-or-mesomorph-what-is-your-body-type

23   Burchard, B (2016) 'Common sense is not always common practice...' [tweet], https://twitter.com/brendonburchard/status/701555535305433094

learning to eat the right quantities of macronutrients (carbs, proteins and fats) from a young age, I only properly understood the science when I started tracking my food intake. Although it took a few weeks to get my head around weighing my food and tracking it in MyFitnessPal (a smartphone app) it is now second nature.

The biggest lesson I learned was that fat is not the enemy. Growing up, I used to buy low fat or fat free versions of everything and believed that eating fat makes you fat. This is a common misperception. I now eat full fat versions of most things and consume plenty of fat in my diet – avocados, nuts, yogurt, oils and so on.

MANAGE YOUR STRESS LEVELS – DECOMPRESS

I rely on exercise to cope with the demands of everyday life. I also give myself the space to breathe, which is really important. I call it decompressing because that is what it feels like to me. It is about getting rid of the worries of my day – through stretching, walking my black Labrador Stella, meditating or journaling. Whatever your outlet, you need to tap into it.

During the first thirty-day block of my body transformation programme I started doing high intensity interval training (HIIIT) to really shift some body fat. It was more about creating new habits than anything else. If you do any exercise consistently enough, you'll see changes. Consistency is king. Once I'd been through the initial habit change, I then started doing some additional work in the gym, where I was focused on shaping and building my body.

This had a different impact on my system altogether. With all the habit changes I had already made, and the new rules I was learning about food and exercise, I realised that in order to build muscle I really had to fuel my body with enough food. This required another significant mental shift.

Many of us go the gym thinking:

- I want to lose weight
- I am going to do lots of cardio
- I am going to starve myself
- I'll have wine instead of food

These thoughts are unhelpful and based on incorrect assumptions. Here are some more useful aims:

- I want to lose fat and build muscle
- I am going to do resistance training to make my body stronger
- I am going to fuel my body with nutritious food
- I'll eat enough to get the most out of my workout

I learned that alcohol is not just empty calories; it's also an anabolic. Our bodies cannot store alcohol. When we drink it, it is quickly absorbed through the small intestine and ends up in our bloodstream. Because it cannot be stored for later use, unlike fats and sugars, it goes to the front of the queue to be dealt with by our liver. Drinking alcohol effectively puts every other digestive process on hold.

DIARISE 'ME TIME' AND DO NOT CANCEL ON YOURSELF

I have to block time in my diary for me. It's impossible to fit everything in otherwise. I diarise my workouts and quality time with my husband and sons. I do this to ensure that I actually enjoy 'me time' and that I am able to decompress properly. It's very rare that I change my diary. This process is one of the most important things to do, but also one of the hardest.

What do you do to decompress? How often do you cancel on yourself? Perhaps it's time to start diarising 'me time'?

SHOW UP AS YOUR BEST SELF

As a leader, regardless of your seniority or role, you have a moral obligation to know the difference between being demanding versus being demeaning. There is a huge difference.

- Being demanding is having extremely high standards and low tolerance for work that falls below them.

- Being demeaning is devaluing other people as human beings, and treating them with disrespect so that they feel worthless.

However, you can learn as much from the bad leaders as you can from the exceptional ones. 'How *not* to lead' was probably the biggest gift my bully gave me. That, and forcing me to build a massive resilience muscle.

Exceptional leaders are highly demanding, but they don't demean others. They operate a *'high challenge – high support'* approach, using both challenge and support equally in a powerful combination. This is what I teach my clients as an accredited Liberating Leadership Practitioner. In order to achieve this, adopt a mindset of 'I'm OK, you're OK' – consistently – even in times of difficulty and poor performance. This is how we create healthy, high-performing, committed teams and individuals, and consistent high achievement and development.

Other combinations of challenge and support generally lead to trouble:

- **Low challenge – low support:** this results in apathy, with low achievement and development.

- **Low challenge – high support:** people are in their comfort zones. Operating this way can be to operate as a hostage to fortune, with people not being the best they can be but being complacently 'good enough'.

- **High challenge – low support:** this is the stress position, the 'sink or swim' version of leadership. If numerous challenges are levelled without support systems (like reinforcement, encouragement or training) then such challenges are unlikely to be well and consistently met.

Exceptional leaders have high expectations of their people and what they can achieve. At the same time, they set attainable goals, use a step-by-step approach, and through explicit communication enable the team and its members to become the best they can be.

When you show up as the best version of you, strive to:

- Reinforce desired behaviours, catch people doing things right, and celebrate wins

- Respect others as individuals and have a positive belief in people

- Be direct, open and honest with others

- Create an environment where everyone can thrive

- Say thank you, often

What kind of leader are you? How do you show up every day?

GET ENERGY FOR LIFE

This involves taking time for yourself, eating well, exercising and working hard on your relationships, your career, and where you want to go with your life. This is important because it impacts everything:

- The way you view the world
- Your tolerance of stress
- Your ability to connect and perform

There is always a bigger picture. I need energy for life because I want to:

- Show up in my business and career fully engaged, inspiring others
- Step into the role of wife and mom, fully present, loving my husband and sons unconditionally
- Connect with my family and friends on a much deeper level

Why do you need energy for life?

IN SUMMARY

It's about raising the bar in all areas of your life. Take one little step at a time and make sure you do things properly. Sometimes we rush through life and expect results instantly. We live in a world where we want things to happen immediately. They don't.

Making your best life a reality will take time and consistency. If you do something consistently for long enough you will get results. I always say: Repeat, repeat, repeat... Life is all about constant, never-ending improvement.

OUTER GAME PROMPTS

- Focus your energy on good things
- Don't negotiate with yourself
- Non-negotiable one: nutrition
- Non-negotiable two: exercise
- De-stress and decompress daily

EIGHT

ROAR! COMMUNICATE WITH IMPACT AND INFLUENCE

'And when I say, "life doesn't happen to you, it happens for you," I really don't know if that's true. I'm just making a conscious choice to perceive challenges as something beneficial so that I can deal with them in the most productive way.'

JIM CARREY

My last and favourite chapter is all about communication. Every single interaction and conversation, whether in person or in writing, creates an experience – good, bad or indifferent. Communication gives our lives meaning.

Explicit, open and transparent communication is the cornerstone of every successful relationship. Your success depends on your ability to communicate with impact and influence, which can be incredibly hard when you're facing a difficult situation.

As this book is about the inner and outer bully, our emphasis in this chapter will be on how to successfully navigate difficult conversations. It all comes down to:

- Winning the inner game – what we think and how we feel
- Winning the outer game – what we say and do

We'll specifically look at how to:

- Identify and call out toxic behaviours
- Set boundaries, and most importantly keep them
- Create win-win outcomes

We cannot always control how others treat us, but we can always choose how we treat others. How you treat people matters a lot. It doesn't mean that you won't sometimes have to have difficult conversations, but always strive to treat others with kindness and respect.

It's never OK to be a bully. Workplaces don't need them. In fact, in 2007 Stanford professor Robert Sutton published a book called *The No Asshole Rule.*[24] He called on companies to set a zero tolerance policy for demeaning and disrespectful

---

24 Sutton, R (2007) *The No Asshole Rule: Building a civilised workplace and surviving one that isn't.* New York: Business Plus.

behaviour. After decades working with companies and doing extensive research, Bob concluded that assholes[25] make us all less productive. He revealed how the costs – to fiscal and mental health – which unpleasant people impose on the people around them, are vast.

What do you think? Should workplaces have a 'no asshole' rule? If so, can you do something about it?

Some sceptics believe that every organisation needs a bully. These people say that the 'no asshole rule' produces cultures that are too polite, at the expense of excellence or quality. According to Sheila Heen, co-author of *Difficult Conversations*,[26] what they're identifying here is the following tension: in polite cultures, if our main goal is not to hurt anybody's feelings, then we don't give each other feedback or point out, 'Actually, we could be doing this a lot better.' The theory is that this leads to standards dropping, and it needs a bully to come along and say, 'What are we thinking? This is stupid.'

To be clear: I am not suggesting we promote polite cultures to the extent where our main goal is not to hurt anyone's feelings. In fact, quite the opposite.

Difficult conversations are inevitable. Excellence is built on explicit communication, constructive feedback and continuous improvement mechanisms. Remember the 'high challenge – high support' approach from Chapter Seven? High performance is all about consistently playing at that pro level in all areas of your life and sustaining this performance over long periods of time.

---

25   www.linkedin.com/pulse/office-without-aholes-adam-grant
26   Stone, D, Patton, B and Heen, S (2011) *Difficult Conversations: How to discuss what matters most.* London: Penguin.

In fact, it is crucial to have difficult conversations (for example, to deal with a performance issue) in which the intentions and impact are positive. They cannot be avoided. However, what if the other person really does have ill intentions – lying, bullying or intentionally derailing the conversation to get what they want? How do you deal with these conversations?

It was only through years of trial and error that I was able to develop effective techniques for dealing with bullies. It's only because I got it wrong so many times that I am able to share some tips and tricks with you. My four-step process for how I navigate difficult conversations is called ROAR.

As with most things, don't expect it work instantly, and it certainly won't work every time. It's an art, not a science. Use it as a guide and recognise that it takes practice to master these things – especially the messy inner game stuff. Sometimes there is just no way you can talk sense into a bully's head. You must know when to walk away. Empower yourself and make it happen. With ROAR, the final piece of the puzzle, my model for living your best life is now complete.

 **1. RECOGNISE**

 **2. OBSERVE**

 **3. ASSERT**

 **4. REDIRECT**

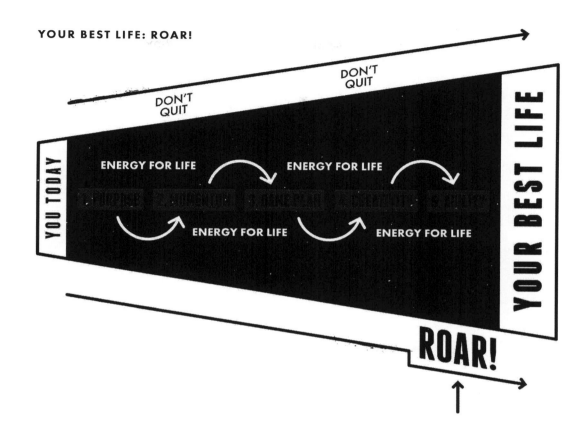

Before we go through ROAR, I want to tell you more about my experience with culture shocks and language barriers.

MY FIVE-YEAR ROLLERCOASTER RIDE

Moving to London in 2004 was a massive culture shock and it opened my eyes to a wide world of possibilities. I was like a rabbit in the headlights. It was supposed to be just a two year stint – the plan was always to return home – but two years became three, four, five and so on, and after almost sixteen years I now call London home (although South Africa will always be where my heart is).

My first year was the toughest; to begin with I hated it. Things got slightly better in year two and before I knew it I had extended my contract for another year, which is also the year we had Heinrich, our oldest son. Becoming a parent completely changed my perspective on life, and we decided to stay in the UK to get our British passports. When people ask me why I choose to live in London when I could live in Cape Town I don't even try to explain. All I say is, 'Life happened.'

Although I didn't completely understand it at the time, I went through a complete transformation in five short years – a new country, a new job, marriage and kids. Throughout this time, I felt confused and struggled to find my voice. I was confused because everything felt so different – people's sense of humour, the way they spoke and expressed themselves, their intonation and use of words, their accents. The South African communication style and our humour is naturally very direct; what you see is what you get. This is very unlike the British, with whom you constantly have to read between the lines. I remember sitting in meeting after meeting not realising someone had just made a joke. I still find it hard sometimes.

To make things worse, English is my second language, after Afrikaans. I grew up in the countryside where I never had to speak English, so I was not fully fluent when I arrived in London. At the time I didn't realise that people are actually very forgiving when it comes to people trying to speak in a second language. Instead, I got frustrated with myself every time I couldn't express myself as well as I could in my mother tongue.

This language barrier, combined with high levels of anxiety, manifested in an outward perception that I lacked confidence, and that I couldn't hold it together. The dominating themes in my feedback appraisals were: 'You wear your heart on your sleeve... You must learn to develop a poker face... You're too emotional.'

Because the feedback contained very little of the 'how' to do these things – my experience with people managers was a bit hit and miss – I had to figure it out myself. Unfortunately, my interpretation was that, in order to progress in a Big Four firm, I had to change who I was. I had to figure out a way to fit into the 'partner mould'. I was too nice to be a leader and garner respect from others. I was convinced that I had to change my personality.

All of this, combined with having kids and going back to work after two stints of maternity leave, knocked my confidence even more. I almost lost myself in the process. Luckily, I came to my senses. It all started to change for me the day I gave myself permission to show up as me: 'Take me or leave me.'

So, among the many lessons learned, I realised two things:

1. Don't try to change who you are for anybody else. If you want to change, do it for yourself.

2. Give yourself permission to show up as you – the 100% authentic version. It's so much more meaningful and fun.

ROAR IN A NUTSHELL

Here is the four-step process summarised.

ROAR: A VISUAL SUMMARY

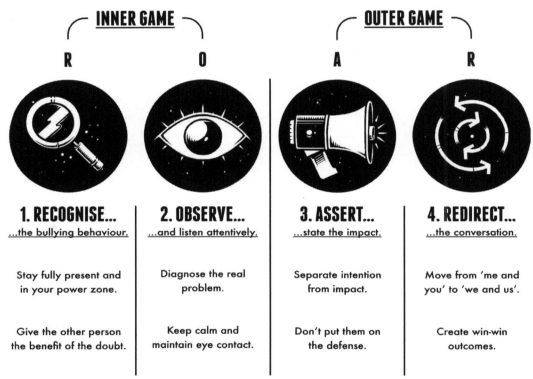

INNER GAME

R · O

OUTER GAME

A · R

1. RECOGNISE...
...the bullying behaviour.

Stay fully present and in your power zone.

Give the other person the benefit of the doubt.

2. OBSERVE...
...and listen attentively.

Diagnose the real problem.

Keep calm and maintain eye contact.

3. ASSERT...
...state the impact.

Separate intention from impact.

Don't put them on the defense.

4. REDIRECT...
...the conversation.

Move from 'me and you' to 'we and us'.

Create win-win outcomes.

Let's explore each step further.

RECOGNISE THE BULLYING BEHAVIOUR

- Stay fully present and in your power zone
- Give the other person the benefit of the doubt

Look out for the signs of bullying behaviour that we covered in Chapter Two. Remember the winner versus loser dynamic? 'I am always right; you are always wrong. I will do anything to prove it.' You're dealing with someone who is aggressive (actively or passively), controlling and often outright rude. At this point, all you probably want to say is: 'I don't know why you feel the need to be so rude and demeaning. Why do you want to humiliate and control everyone?'

DON'T. STAY FULLY PRESENT AND IN YOUR POWER ZONE

Once you've assessed the situation and that it's safe to carry on, try to stay fully present and in your power zone. What do I mean by your power zone? Power is having ownership and authority over your thinking, emotions, words, actions and behaviours. They are *yours*.

Remember 'Think – Feel – Say – Act' from Chapter Six? These are the only four things that we can ever have any power over. Your thoughts and feelings (the inner game) are your private powers, while your words and actions (outer game) are your public powers. Your job is to turn these into your four superpowers.

You have no control over whether someone likes you or not. It's part of their decision-making process; what they think and feel about themselves, in relation to what you're saying. All of this is their inner game that you have no control over.

This realisation is liberating. If you can see that you only have power over your own thoughts, feelings, words and actions, you can take ownership of these four things and let everything else go. If you take responsibility for what you think, feel, say and do, other people cannot have authority over you or influence you unless you allow them to. Nobody can drive you crazy unless you give them the keys.

Once you accept this, you can show up as your true self, and become more authentic as a result.

I would have saved myself so much agony if I'd learned early on to care less about what others thought of me and been myself more often. I would also have stopped trying to please others all the time. I used to be such a people pleaser, and in fact I still am; old habits die hard.

Having this awareness gives you the perfect opportunity to prime your brain properly and reframe your thoughts if necessary. You will have to do it quickly – 'think on your feet' – as the bully has probably caught you off guard. Inflicting narcissistic injuries when someone least expects it is one of the bully's trademark moves. Be aware that you will probably also be experiencing neural dissonance by now, because the sudden shock to your system will have activated the stress response centre in the brain. All your brain wants to do is fight, freeze or flight.

Don't go there. Stay fully present. Breathe.

It's hard to keep listening to someone who is shouting, demeaning and irrational, but remember that you have four amazing superpowers within your gift.

Don't switch off. Figure out how you are going to use your superpowers.

GIVE THE OTHER PERSON THE BENEFIT OF THE DOUBT

Instead of jumping to conclusions about what the other person is thinking and feeling, stay neutral. Recognise that each party has unique opinions, attitudes, beliefs, values and identities. Every single one of us has a unique perspective on ourselves, others and the world. Nobody else shares your perspective. The bully will try everything in their power to control your perspective, but the moment you stop trying to control theirs, they will not be able to control yours.

Giving the other person the benefit of the doubt is especially hard if what the other person is saying and doing goes against your own beliefs and values, which is often the case when you're dealing with a bully. This is a realistic dilemma, but as we saw in Chapter Three, the worst things you can do are to fight back in the moment or to do nothing over time. Most bullies have been playing this dangerous game for a very long time and by getting defensive or ignoring them you're playing right into their hands. You're basically agreeing to play their power game using their rules. You're relinquishing your own power.

Try not to fall into this trap. Maintain the 'I'm OK, you're OK' mindset we discussed in Chapter Three.

OBSERVE AND LISTEN ATTENTIVELY

- Diagnose the real problem
- Keep calm and maintain eye contact

Remember I told you in Chapter One that, for a very long time, I believed that I was the problem? If at all possible, please try not to fall into the same trap. Recognise when you're doing this – are you trying to justify the bully's behaviour? There are a lot of reasons why you might do this: fear, a desire to please others, a need to prove yourself; or you may have crippling self-doubt, limiting beliefs and excuses. The list goes on. The only way to diagnose the real problem is to try to understand the other person's perspective.

Always remember: your truth is not *the* truth. Assume you don't know the other person's truth. Try to move away from an 'us versus them' argumentative mindset in which:

- We blame them – they are the problem
- They blame us – we are the problem

It doesn't help. Trust me, I've made this mistake so many times. I still do sometimes, especially when I am tired, run down and when Scar rears his head. Recognise that we all see the world differently; we all have different stories. However, clearly the reason that this difficult conversation is happening at all is because there is a problem. Or at least, someone has a problem. It is rarely personal, so don't make it about you.

Keep an open mind, give the other person the benefit of the doubt and be curious.

Now that you're ready to respond, the conversation can turn into an opportunity to learn. You're able to ask questions to understand the other person's truth.

KEEP CALM AND MAINTAIN EYE CONTACT THROUGHOUT

Pause... Stop and think.

This is your opportunity, even if it's just a split second, to pause and get your ducks in a row before you say or do something. Take a breath. Compose yourself. Visualise yourself with authority, standing in your power, confident and ready to engage in a two-way conversation.

ASSERT AND STATE THE IMPACT

- Separate intention from impact
- Don't put them on the defensive

Remember, you don't know the other person's intentions or what they're thinking and feeling. It's possible that they don't even understand this themselves. By lashing out they show how little control they have over their feelings and emotions and that's why they become threatening and abusive.

Regardless, don't assume you know the reasons for their behaviour. If you are telling them about their intentions (eg 'Why do you feel the need to be so demeaning?') and their character (eg 'Your behaviour is unprofessional and unacceptable') they are going to argue with you. Trust me, I've been there, done that.

Be curious. Now the conversation can move to, 'Help me understand,' which creates a different dynamic. Ask, 'What makes you say that?' instead of, 'Why did you feel the need to say that?' (the latter is likely to put them on the back foot).

Instead describe the impact. Sometimes bullies are not aware of the effects of their behaviour. In their world they are trying to get their point across, but they don't see how upsetting, demeaning and unprofessional their behaviour is, and the ripple effect it can have throughout the team.

DON'T PUT THEM ON THE DEFENSIVE

This is where you'll need a skilful balance of questioning (eg 'Help me understand') – intentions – and asserting (eg 'This is how it makes me feel') – impact. This strategy is much more likely to lead to a productive conversation and solve the problem – if it is solvable.

Flatter them if you have to. Yes, really. The thing that I hate doing, but do anyway, is stroking overblown egos. It softens the narcissistic blow – rightly or wrongly – and it puts you at an advantage. Show your admiration and interest in them and their talents; it will make them want to hear more. You may be thinking, 'But what if the person is just stubborn and wants to pick a fight? How do you deal with them?' It's your job to help them understand the impact they're having. If you get this balance right, you can become incredibly influential.

However, if they are unable to acknowledge their impact and how their behaviour is part of the problem, this may be the clearest sign yet that the situation is unsolvable. The story in the bully's head goes something like this is: 'The end justifies the means. It was important to get my point across. So what if some people's feelings were hurt? They need to grow up. I am the boss. Yes, I am a brash bastard, but I get away with it because I get results.' Don't try to reason with this kind of bully; either escalate the issue or walk away. It's not worth your time and energy to fight it. At the end of this chapter, I discuss the legal options available to you, if your actions are getting you nowhere.

REDIRECT THE CONVERSATION

- Move from 'me and you' to 'we' and 'us'
- Create win-win outcomes

In meeting after meeting I was told that my team wasn't performing or delivering to the right level. I was getting more and more frustrated by the constant unwarranted criticism. It was starting to feel like a personal assault.

'Breathe Marilise, just breathe,' I told myself. 'He is just a bad communicator. He has always done it this way. Don't let it grind you down. You are bigger than this.' In the beginning, I was defensive and shouted back, which got me nowhere. Sometimes I just took it and said nothing. That got me nowhere either. On other occasions, I stood up and walked away.

Then I discovered the power of 'we'. I asked very calmly for his help. I asked him to help me understand how this was helping 'us' move closer to the delivery of the project in question. This helped to defuse the situation.

He was silent. I was stunned, thinking, 'Is this all that was needed? Simply interrupting the pattern?' I asked him to clarify our vision, so we were clear on our objectives, and so that we were able to come to an agreement on the goal we were working towards.

Moving the conversation from 'me and you' to 'we' changed the focus to the desired outcome and how 'we' could be successful. I realised that a mutual understanding was enough to quiet the critic and that therefore we were in a better position to pull in the same direction – occasionally, at least.

CREATE WIN-WIN OUTCOMES

Our ability to communicate with impact and to influence others is crucial. However, unlike your four superpowers (thoughts, feelings, words and actions) – the capacity you have within you – you don't have any external influence. Influence comes from how you use the superpowers.

You can only persuade someone if they allow you to persuade them, which means they have to persuade themselves first. This is exactly what you're trying to do here. You're trying to persuade the other person that a different outcome is desirable.

Achieving win-win outcomes means gaining the help, cooperation and commitment of others, often with no formal authority. Unfortunately, the natural way we communicate and our learned habits mean that we can inadvertently make the influencing process more difficult and less successful than it can be.

Positive influencing skills help you gain the cooperation of others and bring them round to your way of thinking without manipulating them. This will boost your effectiveness, professional impact and personal credibility.

How influential are you currently in your relationships and career? In which areas of your life do you wish you had more influence right now?

WHAT IF YOUR ACTIONS ARE GETTING YOU NOWHERE?

I highlighted in Chapter Three how less than 5% of survey respondents reported improved behaviour after they confronted their bully. However, if you use ROAR, I am confident that you're well positioned to tame the bully inside and out. By mastering my four-step ROAR process you will not only minimise your daily workplace ructions, but also make it a happier, kinder place to work – for everyone.

The reality is that we deal with 'accidental' bullies every day, and some days we become them when we're stressed, tired or unhappy; this is just life. However, never underestimate the value of a face-to-face conversation. Conversations are catalysts for change. People often ask me: 'Marilise, how do you change workplace culture?' and I always say: 'One conversation at a time.'

However, if you're dealing with an impossible bully, you are going to come out on the other side as the loser, mentally beaten and bruised. If this is your reality today, now is the time to stop, to get honest with yourself and to ask for help.

ASK FOR HELP

Remember: it's not your responsibility to deal with a bully. Bullying demands systemic and legal intervention by your employer and by HR. This is much more than a legal intervention. Escalating it is the right – and moral – thing to do.

Remember the Amnesty International case, and the results from my own research study? How more than half of survey respondents didn't inform HR largely for fear of retribution? How a quarter of respondents said HR did nothing despite requests for support? How only 10% said HR resolved or attempted to resolve the situation positively, completely or partially? How the rest said that it was too late?

Ask for help before it's too late. Here are my four top tips for legally protecting yourself:

TIP 1: KNOW WHO YOU CAN AND CANNOT TRUST

Review your documented evidence and if you need further evidence ask around discreetly if colleagues have had similar experiences. If they say yes, you have a better chance of being taken seriously. You might even ask colleagues you trust if they'd be willing to support you in taking action.

This is an extremely risky move. Why? First of all, the bully must not find out what you're up to – it will be career suicide – so be very clear about who your allies are. The reality is that the vast majority of people are too scared to speak up; they want to protect their reputation and rather leave quietly.

TIP 2: TAKE TIME OUT – IT'S A SIGN OF STRENGTH, NOT WEAKNESS

It is critical that at some point you check in with yourself. How is your health?

Acknowledging that work-related stress is negatively impacting your mental and physical health, and getting signed off work, is not a sign of weakness. In fact it is quite the opposite. I wish I'd realised this sooner. I refused to even entertain the idea of going to the doctors and getting signed off. To me this would have meant that he'd won. I couldn't let that happen. We all know how that story ended.

By going on sick leave, you are being kind to yourself. By removing yourself from the situation, you can regain perspective and consider your options.

Forget about the bully and their shenanigans. If anything, you've sent them a clear message: that you are not their slave.

TIP 3: KNOW YOUR RIGHTS

If you have taken your appeals higher by raising a formal grievance and your supervisor or HR team have listened carefully to your concerns and even intervened on your behalf, you're in a good place. Keep working with them and providing updates on the situation. If you have tried interventions at every level, and the supervisor or the system are unresponsive to your needs, you've truly done all you can. Your needs aren't likely to be met. The system itself might be stuck in a toxic cycle, which means your bully is merely a symptom of a toxic culture.

Unfortunately, some organisations are prone to abusing non-disclosure agreements (NDAs) to intimidate whistle-blowers and conceal harassment and discrimination, including sexual assault, bullying, physical threats and racism. My research indicates that organisations use NDAs extensively to silence victims of bullying. This is kept out of the sight of the public. Companies are throwing money at the problem to make it go away. It is a silent epidemic, and it has to stop.

Make sure you know your legal rights by speaking to an employment lawyer early on. Only 2% of targets took legal action, according to my research. Over half said the reason they didn't take legal action was that they were too mentally and physically exhausted to fight their bully. Others said they feared for their reputation or that they couldn't justify the legal costs.

TIP 4: LEAVE

Leaving a job can feel impossible, but if you've tried to make things better and still feel miserable then choosing to stay will mean continued misery. That's why it is time to take control and leave.

Know this: there are no accidents. Everyone comes into your life for a reason, a lesson or a blessing. Thank the toxic people in your life. Why thank them? They taught you how you must not be treated. They showed you how not to treat others. They showed you how to move on. They gave you strength and character and they expanded your heart. Don't let them stop you from becoming your greatest self.

IN SUMMARY

For me, pursuing my best life has a lot to with my daily (high performance) habits and maintaining a healthy balance in everything I do. This includes striving to be a healthy 5 on the Narcissism Spectrum Scale.

What I've learned about myself is that I will always have a tendency to push myself to the limit, probably until the day I die. Nature and nurture mean that I'll probably always live life to extremes, and although this attitude serves me well most of the time, there are still days when I lack willpower and feel overwhelmed, anxious and weak. On these days Scar is having a field day and I have to be particularly careful with my choices.

There are days when I have to catch myself, take a deep breath and ask: 'Marilise, can you do it today? Can you make it through today, just today, and tomorrow we'll reconsider?' Doing this exercise instantly releases an enormous amount of pressure and makes me feel a lot lighter. It helps me to be more present and it helps me to be kinder to myself.

I used to have an amazing boss who always said, 'Perfect is the enemy of good enough,' and although it didn't really sink in at the time, years later I fully understand and appreciate the significance of his advice. Unfortunately, it took a not-so-amazing boss – one who was never satisfied with anything – to make me realise that perfection is indeed the enemy of good enough. In workplaces it stifles innovation and destroys team morale. It also messes with people's heads – we start to believe that we are the problem.

Only two changes are possible: something new or positive is going to come into your life, or something new is going to come from within. Give it time; it will take as long as it takes. It is a process. When you plant new seeds there is a process required for the seeds to grow into a beautiful flower or tree. It can take days, months or years.

Live in the moment, and remember:

- Progress, not perfection
- Work hard, play hard and be kind

Your best life awaits on the other side of your biggest obstacle. It is my wish that you will find the inner strength and courage to pursue your dreams and make your best life a reality. Step forward and find your ROAR!

FIND YOUR ROAR! PROMPTS

- Hold on to your power
- Give yourself permission
- Be your authentic self
- Choose to be kind
- Have a go... find your ROAR!

MY WORKPLACE CULTURE SURVEY: QUESTIONS

1. What country do you work in?

2. Which of the following best describes the principal industry of your organisation?

3. Roughly how many employees currently work for your organisation globally?

4. What is your level in the organisation?

5. Have you ever been a Target or Witness to repeated mistreatment in the workplace, through verbal abuse, threatening conduct or work interference, to the point where it harmed the Target's health and caused distress (financial, emotional or otherwise)?

6. In how many different work situations and organisations were you the Target or Witness of mistreatment?

7. Please indicate if you are answering the remaining questions from the perspective of the Target or the Witness. (Note: If you would like to answer from the perspective of both the Target and the Witness, please complete the survey from your preferred perspective first, and then complete it again from the other perspective.)

8. Please describe the emotions you felt when the mistreatment occurred. Select all that apply.

9. How frequently did you feel these emotions?

10. What were your most common responses to the mistreatment?

11. Gender of Target.

12. Gender of Witness(es).

13. What was the longest period you were the Target or Witness of the mistreatment? Please state in years and months (eg three years, four months).

14. Who was targeted for the mistreatment?

15. Did the mistreatment occur face-to-face, online (or both)? Select all that apply.

16. Was the mistreatment discriminatory in nature? Select all that apply.

17. Gender of the principal Harasser (or instigator).

18. Where did the Harasser work?

19. Did the Harasser work alone, or were there several people involved in the mistreatment?

20. The Harasser's seniority relative to the Target.

21. The Harasser's seniority relative to the Witness.

22. Describe the mistreatment. Select all categories that apply.

23. Has the environment (workplace culture) made it easier or harder for the Harasser to mistreat the Target(s)?

24. What impact did the mistreatment have on you, if any? Select all that apply.

25. What impact on the organisation, if any, did you observe? Select all that apply.

26. What stopped the mistreatment?

27. If the Target took legal action, what was the outcome (eg the Target was paid off and signed a non-disclosure agreement)?

28. If the Target didn't take legal action, why was this?

29. How did the following parties respond to the mistreatment? Target's Supervisor, Manager or Executive.

30. How did the following parties respond to the mistreatment? Human Resources, Ethics & Compliance, Speak Up helpline and so on.

31. How did the following parties respond to the mistreatment? Harasser's Supervisor, Manager or Executive.

32. Were there any positive outcomes from the mistreatment? Please describe them.

ABOUT THE CREATIVE

Very soon after I decided to write this book, I realised that my cousin Christi du Toit,[1] a talented illustrator and designer based in Cape Town, was the perfect person to design the cover. Here is the story, in his words, of his stunning artwork and designs:

> *My approach to creating the artwork and designs for ROAR! was to convey the underlying theme through striking key visuals, as well as more subtle hints throughout. The cover shows a character standing confidently, which is further emphasised by their shadow taking the form of a lion. The lion ties in directly with the title of the book, but it also tells a story of confidence, assertiveness and leadership. The back cover shows the same character 'roaring' into a microphone. The sole purpose of a microphone is to make your voice louder, so that you can be heard – a strong visual metaphor.*

---

1   http://christidutoit.co.za

153

We chose to stylise the character in a way that it is loosely based on Marilise, the author, but also avoids too many defining features which helps with relatability – if you're reading this book, this character could be you! The overall artwork style was inspired by vintage revolution posters with strong, impactful graphics, as a big theme for those posters was to stand up to make a change.

Though a subtle aspect, the worn out, textured look that was applied to the diagram designs was chosen to communicate the idea of something that has been through rough times, but which is still standing. Something that is tough enough to withstand the wear and tear that the world around it presents, not unlike someone who has dealt with a bully and came out undefeated.

ACKNOWLEDGEMENTS

How do I possibly thank every single person I spoke to since Friday 9 November 2018, the day I (consciously) decided to write a book? Every conversation shaped my ideas and brought me one step closer to making *ROAR!* a reality.

I'll start with Heinie. You were the first person to know and who calmly told me, 'You've got this my love,' after I realised what I'd done and panicked. Your faith in me means the world.

I'd like to say thank you to Heinrich and Andreas, for your patience and understanding when doing fun things without Mom while she's writing her book. I know it has taken forever in your eyes. You guys are awesome, and I promise to make it up to you.

To Scott, for helping us to raise the boys and run a household. I honestly don't know what we would've done without you. Most of all, thank you for your positive energy and listening patiently to me sharing my ideas for *ROAR!* and more (often at the crack of dawn).

To Divvie and Karin. Dad, Mom, for welcoming me to your world when you were still kids yourselves and for loving me unconditionally every day since. I will forever treasure the memories of driving in dad's champagne Audi 4 singing Neil Diamond and Bruce Springsteen songs at the top of my lungs. Thank you for a barefoot, carefree childhood in the countryside and, above all, for making me believe that anything is possible.

To Elsabet and Kara, my two beautiful sisters. Ella, for the gift of inner beauty and self-love. Kara, for reminding me that if I change only one person's life with this book, it's worth it.

To Colette Pienaar, my 'all-in-one' person – transformation coach, social media marketing guru and dearest friend – for helping me to get into the best shape of my life, mentally and physically, and cheering me on every day.

To Jane Frankland, who was sent to me by the Universe at just the right time. Thank you for helping me to take back my power and for supporting me every step of the way. You are living proof that 'we rise by lifting others'.

To Tia Tokoro, for reminding me what's important in life, always prioritising your beautiful girls and for being one of the strongest women I know. I have so much admiration and respect for you, my friend.

To Siobhan Costello, for helping me finish *ROAR!* and the 'tough love' you showed me when my imposter got the better of me. Also, to the rest of the amazing Rethink Press team – thank you for believing in me from day one and for the solid support along the way.

To my cousin Christi, for the mind-blowing graphics. It was such an honour to work with you and to get to know the real you. You have been blessed with an incredible talent and I am excited to see what the future holds for you.

To Ali Stewart, for the gift of Liberating Leadership and being an incredible mentor and friend ever since. I admire and appreciate your serenity, sincerity and generosity. Also, for my beautiful Foreword, thank you dearest Ali.

To everyone who helped me shape my survey. In particular, Chris Parke, for making me realise that I had to do a survey (I was desperate not to), and David Moloney for providing the much needed 'logic checks', quality assurance and moral support along the way.

To everyone who offered to read the final draft of *ROAR!* and for the kind words.

To everyone who completed my survey and shared their story – in person or online. I can't name you, but you know who you are. Thank you for being so brave and showing strength in vulnerability.

To my online personal development gurus – Brendon Burchard, Dean Graziosi, Tony Robbins, Vishan Lakhiani and John Assaraf. I wish to meet you all one day to personally thank you for inspiring me to live my why and pursue my best life.

Finally, to my readers. Thank you for reading *ROAR!* Please join me on my mission to bring more kindness to the workplace, in fact, across society as a whole.

THE AUTHOR

Marilise de Villiers is the founder and CEO of Marilise de Villiers Basson Consulting. She's a mover and shaker in the cybersecurity space and is changing the current landscape. She believes that people are the greatest asset when it comes to keeping organisations and society safe. Her approach is to coach and support cybersecurity executives on the design and delivery of effective people and behavioural change strategies.

Through her consulting, training and coaching she is on a mission to create high-performing cultures. Integral to this work is her conviction that the workplace today is in dire need of more kindness, clarity and engagement around a common vision in order to deliver world class results. Looking past our differences and seeing the good in others can make our working lives a lot happier, more fulfilling, productive and profitable.

Marilise's one-to-one clients usually come to her when they are facing challenging situations at work that seem unsolvable. They feel isolated and alone and are simply tired of firefighting; they need a simple approach that will help them take back control. Working with Marilise brings clarity on the person they wish to become and the legacy they wish to leave behind.

Here are five fun facts about the author:

1. Her star sign is the lovable Leo. She's one through and through – exuberant, loyal, self-confident, with big ideas and an even bigger heart. She believes that miracles happen every day – we just have to stop and see them.

2. She has a strong artistic streak and used to make and sell birthday cards as a student.

3. Her lifelong dream is to have her own flower farm. While working on this dream, a fresh box of flowers is the highlight of her week.

4. She loves a glass of ice-cold Sauvignon Blanc (preferably South African).

5. Her drug of choice is exercise. This is also her creative outlet; she wrote significant parts of this book on a bicycle or treadmill when the endorphins were flowing.

CONTACT

You can find Marilise online at:

🌐 www.marilise-de-villiers.com

in www.linkedin.com/in/marilise-de-villiers-9184521a

𝕏 @marilise77

f www.facebook.com/marilisedevilliers

📷 www.instagram.com/marilisebasson

Printed in Great Britain
by Amazon